ARMS AND THE MAN

ARMS AND THE MAN

An Anti-Romantic Comedy in Three Acts

by

BERNARD SHAW

with an Introduction
and notes by

A. C. WARD

'*Arma virumque cano.*'

Longman Group Ltd
London · New York · Toronto
in association with
Constable and Co Ltd
London

LONGMAN GROUP LIMITED
London

*Associated companies, branches and representatives
throughout the world*

© Longman Group Ltd 1955

*This edition first published 1955
Sixteenth impression *1973*

ISBN 0 582 53254 X

*Printed in Hong Kong by
Sheck Wah Tong Printing Press*

CONTENTS

By A. C. WARD

PREFACE TO *PLAYS PLEASANT*
(1898)

READERS of the discourse with which the preceding volume commences will remember that I turned my hand to play-writing when a great deal of talk about "the New Drama," followed by the actual establishment of a "New Theatre" (the Independent), threatened to end in the humiliating discovery that the New Drama, in England at least, was a figment of the revolutionary imagination. This was not to be endured. I had rashly taken up the case; and rather than let it collapse I manufactured the evidence.

Man is a creature of habit. You cannot write three plays and then stop. Besides, the New movement did not stop. In 1894, Florence Farr, who had already produced Ibsen's Rosmersholm, was placed in command of the Avenue Theatre in London for a season on the new lines by Miss A. E. F. Horniman, who had family reasons for not yet appearing openly as a pioneer-manageress. There were, as available New Dramatists, myself, discovered by the Independent Theatre (at my own suggestion); Dr John Todhunter, who had been discovered before (his play The Black Cat had been one of the Independent's successes); and Mr W. B. Yeats, a genuine discovery. Dr Todhunter supplied A Comedy of Sighs: Mr Yeats, The Land of Heart's Desire. I, having nothing but unpleasant plays in my desk, hastily completed a first attempt at a pleasant one, and called it Arms and The Man, taking the title from the first line of Dryden's Virgil. It passed for a success, the applause on the first night being as promising as could be wished; and it ran from the 21st of April to the 7th of July. To witness it the public paid £1777 : 5 : 6, an average of £23:2:5 per representation (including nine matinées). A publisher receiving £1700 for a book would have made a satisfactory profit: experts in West End theatrical management will contemplate that figure with a grim smile.

In the autumn of 1894 I spent a few weeks in Florence, where

I occupied myself with the religious art of the Middle Ages and
its destruction by the Renascence. From a former visit to Italy
on the same business I had hurried back to Birmingham to discharge my duties as musical critic at the Festival there. On that
occasion a very remarkable collection of the works of our British
"pre-Raphaelite" painters was on view. I looked at these, and
then went into the Birmingham churches to see the windows of
William Morris and Burne-Jones. On the whole, Birmingham
was more hopeful than the Italian cities; for the art it had to shew
me was the work of living men, whereas modern Italy had, as far
as I could see, no more connection with Giotto than Port Said
has with Ptolemy. Now I am no believer in the worth of any mere
taste for art that cannot produce what it professes to appreciate.
When my subsequent visit to Italy found me practising the playwright's craft, the time was ripe for a modern pre-Raphaelite play.
Religion was alive again, coming back upon men, even upon
clergymen, with such power that not the Church of England itself
could keep it out. Here my activity as a Socialist had placed me
on sure and familiar ground. To me the members of the Guild of
St Matthew were no more "High Church clergymen," Dr
Clifford no more "an eminent Nonconformist divine," than I
was to them "an infidel." There is only one religion, though there
are a hundred versions of it. We all had the same thing to say;
and though some of us cleared our throats to say it by singing
revolutionary lyrics and republican hymns, we thought nothing
of singing them to the music of Sullivan's Onward Christian
Soldiers or Haydn's God Preserve the Emperor.

Now unity, however desirable in political agitations, is fatal
to drama; for every drama must present a conflict. The end may
be reconciliation or destruction; or, as in life itself, there may be
no end; but the conflict is indispensable: no conflict, no drama.
Certainly it is easy to dramatize the prosaic conflict of Christian
Socialism with vulgar Unsocialism: for instance, in Widowers'
Houses, the clergyman, who does not appear on the stage at all,
is the real antagonist of the slum landlord. But the obvious con-

flicts of unmistakeable good with unmistakeable evil can only supply the crude drama of villain and hero, in which some absolute point of view is taken, and the dissentients are treated by the dramatist as enemies to be piously glorified or indignantly vilified. In such cheap wares I do not deal. Even in my unpleasant propagandist plays I have allowed every person his or her own point of view, and have, I hope, to the full extent of my understanding of him, been as sympathetic with Sir George Crofts as with any of the more genial and popular characters in the present volume. To distil the quintessential drama from pre-Raphaelitism, medieval or modern, it must be shewn at its best in conflict with the first broken, nervous, stumbling attempts to formulate its own revolt against itself as it develops into something higher. A coherent explanation of any such revolt, addressed intelligibly and prosaically to the intellect, can only come when the work is done, and indeed *done with*: that is to say, when the development, accomplished, admitted, and assimilated, is a story of yesterday. Long before any such understanding can be reached, the eyes of men begin to turn towards the distant light of the new age Discernible at first only by the eyes of the man of genius, it must be focussed by him on the speculum of a work of art, and flashed back from that into the eyes of the common man. Nay, the artist himself has no other way of making himself conscious of the ray: it is by a blind instinct that he keeps on building up his masterpieces until their pinnacles catch the glint of the unrisen sun. Ask him to explain himself prosaically, and you find that he "writes like an angel and talks like poor Poll," and is himself the first to make that epigram at his own expense. John Ruskin has told us clearly enough what is in the pictures of Carpaccio and Bellini: let him explain, if he can, where we shall be when the sun that is caught by the summits of the work of his favorite Tintoretto, of his aversion Rembrandt, of Mozart, of Beethoven and Wagner, of Blake and of Shelley, shall have reached the valleys. Let Ibsen explain, if he can, why the building of churches and happy homes is not the ultimate destiny of Man, and why, to thrill the unsatisfied younger generations, he must mount beyond it to heights that now seem unspeakably giddy and dreadful to him, and from which the first climbers must fall and dash themselves to pieces. He cannöt explain it: he can only shew it to you as a vision in the magic glass of his artwork; so that you may catch his presentiment and make what you can of it. And this is the function that raises dramatic art above imposture and pleasure hunting, and enables the playwright to be something more than a skilled liar and pandar.

Here, then, was the higher but vaguer and timider vision, the incoherent, mischievous, and even ridiculous unpracticalness, which offered me a dramatic antagonist for the clear, bold, sure, sensible, benevolent, salutarily shortsighted Christian Socialist idealism. I availed myself of it in Candida, the drunken scene in which has been much appreciated, I am told, in Aberdeen. I purposely contrived the play in such a way as to make the expenses of representation insignificant; so that, without pretending that I could appeal to a very wide circle of playgoers, I could reasonably sound a few of our more enlightened managers as to an experiment with half a dozen afternoon performances. They admired the play generously: indeed I think that if any of them had been young enough to play the poet, my proposal might have been acceded to, in spite of many incidental difficulties. Nay, if only I had made the poet a cripple, or at least blind, so as to combine an easier disguise with a larger claim for sympathy, something might have been done. Richard Mansfield, who had, with apparent ease, made me quite famous in America by his productions of my plays, went so far as to put the play actually into rehearsal before he would confess himself beaten by the physical difficulties of the part. But they did beat him; and Candida did not see the footlights until my old ally the Independent Theatre, making a propagandist tour through the provinces with A Doll's House, added Candida to its repertory, to the great astonishment of its audiences.

In an idle moment in 1895 I began the little scene called The

Man of Destiny, which is hardly more than a bravura piece to display the virtuosity of the two principal performers.

In the meantime I had devoted the spare moments of 1896 to the composition of two more plays, only the first of which appears in this volume. You Never Can Tell was an attempt to comply with many requests for a play in which the much paragraphed "brilliancy" of Arms and The Man should be tempered by some consideration for the requirements of managers in search of fashionable comedies for West End theatres. I had no difficulty in complying, as I have always cast my plays in the ordinary practical comedy form in use at all the theatres; and far from taking an unsympathetic view of the popular preference for fun, fashionable dresses, a little music, and even an exhibition of eating and drinking by people with an expensive air, attended by an if-possible-comic waiter, I was more than willing to shew that the drama can humanize these things as easily as they, in the wrong hands, can dehumanize the drama. But as often happens it was easier to do this than to persuade those who had asked for it that they had indeed got it. A chapter in Cyril Maude's history of the Haymarket Theatre records how the play was rehearsed there, and why I withdrew it. And so I reached the point at which, as narrated in the preface to the Unpleasant volume, I resolved to avail myself of my literary expertness to put my plays before the public in my own way.

It will be noticed that I have not been driven to this expedient by any hostility on the part of our managers. I will not pretend that the modern actor-manager's talent as player can in the nature of things be often associated with exceptional critical insight. As a rule, by the time a manager has experience enough to make him as safe a judge of plays as a Bond Street dealer is of pictures, he begins to be thrown out in his calculations by the slow but constant change of public taste, and by his own growing conservatism. But his need for new plays is so great, and the few accredited authors are so little able to keep pace with their commissions, that he is always apt to overrate rather than to underrate his discoveries in the way of new pieces by new authors. An original work by a man of genius like Ibsen may, of course, baffle him as it baffles many professed critics; but in the beaten path of drama no unacted works of merit, suitable to his purposes, have been discovered; whereas the production, at great expense, of very faulty plays written by novices (not "backers") is by no means an unknown event. Indeed, to anyone who can estimate, even vaguely, the complicated trouble, the risk of heavy loss, and the initial expense and thought, involved by the production of a play, the ease with which dramatic authors, known and unknown, get their works performed must needs seem a wonder.

Only, authors must not expect managers to invest many thousands of pounds in plays, however fine (or the reverse), which will clearly not attract perfectly commonplace people. Playwriting and theatrical management, on the present commercial basis, are businesses like other businesses, depending on the patronage of great numbers of very ordinary customers. When the managers and authors study the wants of these customers, they succeed: when they do not, they fail. A public-spirited manager, or an author with a keen artistic conscience, may choose to pursue his business with the minimum of profit and the maximum of social usefulness by keeping as close as he can to the highest marketable limit of quality, and constantly feeling for an extension of that limit through the advance of popular culture. An unscrupulous manager or author may aim simply at the maximum of profit with the minimum of risk. These are the opposite poles of our system, represented in practice by our first rate managements at the one end, and the syndicates which exploit pornographic farces at the other. Between them there is plenty of room for most talents to breathe freely: at all events there is a career, no harder of access than any cognate career, for all qualified playwrights who bring the manager what his customers want and understand, or even enough of it to induce them to swallow at the same time a great deal that they neither want nor understand; for the public is touchingly humble in such matters.

For all that, the commercial limits are too narrow for our social welfare. The theatre is growing in importance as a social organ. Bad theatres are as mischievous as bad schools or bad churches; for modern civilization is rapidly multiplying the class to which the theatre is both school and church. Public and private life become daily more theatrical: the modern Kaiser, Dictator, President or Prime Minister is nothing if not an effective actor; all newspapers are now edited histrionically; and the records of our law courts shew that the stage is affecting personal conduct to an unprecedented extent, and affecting it by no means for the worse, except in so far as the theatrical education of the persons concerned has been romantic: that is, spurious, cheap, and vulgar. The truth is that dramatic invention is the first effort of man to become intellectually conscious. No frontier can be marked between drama and history or religion, or between acting and conduct, nor any distinction made between them that is not also the distinction between the masterpieces of the great dramatic poets and the commonplaces of our theatrical seasons. When this chapter of science is convincingly written, the national importance of the theatre will be as unquestioned as that of the army, the fleet, the Church, the law, and the schools.

For my part, I have no doubt that the commercial limits should be overstepped, and that the highest prestige, with a financial position of reasonable security and comfort, should be attainable in theatrical management by keeping the public in constant touch with the highest achievements of dramatic art. Our managers will not dissent to this: the best of them are so willing to get as near that position as they can without ruining themselves, that they can all point to honorable losses incurred through aiming "over the heads of the public," and will no doubt risk such loss again, for the sake of their reputation as artists, as soon as a few popular successes enable them to afford it. But even if it were possible for them to educate the nation at their own private cost, why should they be expected to do it? There are much stronger objections to the pauperization of the public by private doles than were ever entertained, even by the Poor Law Commissioners of 1834, to the pauperization of private individuals by public doles. If we want a theatre which shall be to the drama what the National Gallery and British Museum are to painting and literature, we can get it by endowing it in the same way. In the meantime there are many possibilities of local activity. Groups of amateurs can form permanent societies and persevere until they develop into professional companies in established repertory theatres. In big cities it should be feasible to form influential committees, preferably without any actors, critics, or playwrights on them, and with as many persons of title as possible, for the purpose of approaching one of the leading local managers with a proposal that they shall, under a guarantee against loss, undertake a certain number of afternoon performances of the class required by the committee, in addition to their ordinary business. If the committee is influential enough, the offer will be accepted. In that case, the first performance will be the beginning of a classic repertory for the manager and his company which every subsequent performance will extend. The formation of the repertory will go hand in hand with the discovery and habituation of a regular audience for it; and it will eventually become profitable for the manager to multiply the number of performances at his own risk. It might even become worth his while to take a second theatre and establish the repertory permanently in it. In the event of any of his classic productions proving a fashionable success, he could transfer it to his fashionable house and make the most of it there. Such managership would carry a knighthood with it; and such a theatre would be the needed nucleus for municipal or national endowment. I make the suggestion quite disinterestedly; for as I am not an academic person, I should not be welcomed as an unacted classic by such a committee; and cases like mine would still leave forlorn hopes like The Independent Theatre its reason for existing. The committee plan, I may remind its critics, has been in operation in London for two hundred years in support of Italian opera.

Returning now to the actual state of things, it is clear that I have no grievance against our theatres. Knowing quite well what I was doing, I have heaped difficulties in the way of the performance of my plays by ignoring the majority of the manager's customers: nay, by positively making war on them. To the actor I have been more considerate, using all my cunning to enable him to make the most of his technical methods; but I have not hesitated on occasion to tax his intelligence very severely, making the stage effect depend not only on *nuances* of execution quite beyond the average skill produced by the routine of the English stage in its present condition, but on a perfectly sincere and straightforward conception of states of mind which still seem cynically perverse to most people, and on a goodhumoredly contemptuous or profoundly pitiful attitude towards ethical conventions which seem to them validly heroic or venerable. It is inevitable that actors should suffer more than most of us from the sophistication of their consciousness by romance; and my view of romance as the great heresy to be swept off from art and life—as the food of modern pessimism and the bane of modern self-respect, is far more puzzling to the performers than it is to the pit. It is hard for an actor whose point of honor it is to be a perfect gentleman, to sympathize with an author who regards gentility as a dishonest folly, and gallantry and chivalry as treasonable to women and stultifying to men.

The misunderstanding is complicated by the fact that actors, in their demonstrations of emotion, have made a second nature of stage custom, which is often very much out of date as a representation of contemporary life. Sometimes the stage custom is not only obsolete, but fundamentally wrong: for instance, in the simple case of laughter and tears, in which it deals too liberally, it is certainly not based on the fact, easily enough discoverable in real life, that we only cry now in the effort to bear happiness, whilst we laugh and exult in destruction, confusion, and ruin.

B

When a comedy is performed, it is nothing to me that the spectators laugh: any fool can make an audience laugh. I want to see how many of them, laughing or grave, are in the melting mood. And this result cannot be achieved, even by actors who thoroughly understand my purpose, except through an artistic beauty of execution unattainable without long and arduous practice, and an intellectual effort which my plays probably do not seem serious enough to call forth.

Beyond the difficulties thus raised by the nature and quality of my work, I have none to complain of. I have come upon no ill will, no inaccessibility, on the part of the very few managers with whom I have discussed it. As a rule I find that the actor-manager is over-sanguine, because he has the artist's habit of underrating the force of circumstances and exaggerating the power of the talented individual to prevail against them; whilst I have acquired the politician's habit of regarding the individual, however talented, as having no choice but to make the most of his circumstances. I half suspect that those managers who have had most to do with me, if asked to name the main obstacle to the performance of my plays, would unhesitatingly and unanimously reply "The author." And I confess that though as a matter of business I wish my plays to be performed, as a matter of instinct I fight against the inevitable misrepresentation of them with all the subtlety needed to conceal my ill will from myself as well as from the manager.

The main difficulty, of course, is the incapacity for serious drama of thousands of playgoers of all classes whose shillings and half guineas will buy as much in the market as if they delighted in the highest art. But with them I must frankly take the superior position. I know that many managers are wholly dependent on them, and that no manager is wholly independent of them; but I can no more write what they want than Joachim can put aside his fiddle and oblige a happy company of beanfeasters with a marching tune on the German concertina. They must keep away from my plays: that is all.

There is no reason, however, why I should take this haughty attitude towards those representative critics whose complaint is that my talent, though not unentertaining, lacks elevation of sentiment and seriousness of purpose. They can find, under the surface-brilliancy for which they give me credit, no coherent thought or sympathy, and accuse me, in various terms and degrees, of an inhuman and freakish wantonness; of preoccupation with "the seamy side of life"; of paradox, cynicism, and eccentricity, reducible, as some contend, to a trite formula of treating bad as good and good as bad, important as trivial and trivial as important, serious as laughable and laughable as serious, and so forth. As to this formula I can only say that if any gentleman is simple enough to think that even a good comic opera can be produced by it, I invite him to try his hand, and see whether anything resembling one of my plays will reward him.

I could explain the matter easily enough if I chose; but the result would be that the people who misunderstand the plays would misunderstand the explanation ten times more. The particular exceptions taken are seldom more than symptoms of the underlying fundamental disagreement between the romantic morality of the critics and the natural morality of the plays. For example, I am quite aware that the much criticized Swiss officer in Arms and The Man is not a conventional stage soldier. He suffers from want of food and sleep; his nerves go to pieces after three days under fire, ending in the horrors of a rout and pursuit; he has found by experience that it is more important to have a few bits of chocolate to eat in the field than cartridges for his revolver. When many of my critics rejected these circumstances as fantastically improbable and cynically unnatural, it was not necessary to argue them into common sense: all I had to do was to brain them, so to speak, with the first half dozen military authorities at hand, beginning with the present Commander in Chief. But when it proved that such unromantic (but all the more dramatic) facts implied to them a denial of the existence of courage, patriotism, faith, hope, and charity, I saw that it was not really mere matter of fact that was at issue between us. One strongly Liberal critic, the late Moy Thomas, who had, in the teeth of a chorus of dissent, received my first play with the most generous encouragement, declared, when Arms and The Man was produced, that I had struck a wanton blow at the cause of liberty in the Balkan Peninsula by mentioning that it was not a matter of course for a Bulgarian in 1885 to wash his hands every day. He no doubt saw soon afterwards the squabble, reported all through Europe, between Stambouloff and an eminent lady of the Bulgarian court who took exception to his neglect of his fingernails. After that came the news of his ferocious assassination, with a description of the room prepared for the reception of visitors by his widow, who draped it with black, and decorated it with photographs of the mutilated body of her husband. Here was a sufficiently sensational confirmation of the accuracy of my sketch of the theatrical nature of the first apings of western civilization by spirited races just emerging from slavery. But it had no bearing on the real issue between my critic and myself, which was, whether the political and religious idealism which had inspired Gladstone to call for the rescue of these Balkan principalities from the despotism of the Turk, and converted miserably enslaved provinces into hopeful and gallant little States, will survive the general onslaught on idealism which is implicit, and indeed explicit, in Arms and The Man and the naturalist plays of the modern school. For my part I hope not; for idealism, which is only a flattering name for romance in politics and morals, is as obnoxious to me as romance in ethics or religion. In spite of a Liberal Revolution or two, I can no longer be satisfied with fictitious morals and fictitious good conduct, shedding fictitious glory on robbery, starvation, disease, crime, drink, war, cruelty, cupidity, and all the other commonplaces of civilization which drive men to the theatre to make foolish pretences that such things are progress, science, morals, religion, patriotism, imperial supremacy, national greatness and all the other names the newspapers call them. On the other hand, I see plenty of good in the world working itself out as fast as the idealists will allow it; and if they would only let it alone and learn to respect reality, which would include the beneficial exercise of respecting themselves, and incidentally respecting me, we should all get along much better and faster. At all events, I do not see moral chaos and anarchy as the alternative to romantic convention; and I am not going to pretend I do merely to please the people who are convinced that the world is held together only by the force of unanimous, strenuous, eloquent, trumpet-tongued lying. To me the tragedy and comedy of life lie in the consequences, sometimes terrible, sometimes ludicrous, of our persistent attempts to found our institutions on the ideals suggested to our imaginations by our half-satisfied passions, instead of on a genuinely scientific natural history. And with that hint as to what I am driving at, I withdraw and ring up the curtain.

Arms and The Man was performed for the first time at the Avenue Theatre, London, on the 21st April 1894, by Alma Murray as Raina, Mrs Charles Calvert as Catherine, Florence Farr as Louka, Yorke Stephens as Bluntschli, A. E. W. Mason as the Russian Officer, Orlando Barnett as Nicola, James Welch as Petkoff, and Bernard Gould (Sir Bernard Partridge) as Sergius.

ARMS AND THE MAN

ACT I

Night: A lady's bedchamber in Bulgaria, in a small town near the Dragoman Pass, late in November in the year 1885. Through an open window with a little balcony a peak of the Balkans, wonderfully white and beautiful in the starlit snow, seems quite close at hand, though it is really miles away. The interior of the room is not like anything to be seen in the west of Europe. It is half rich Bulgarian, half cheap Viennese. Above the head of the bed, which stands against a little wall cutting off the left hand corner of the room, is a painted wooden shrine, blue and gold, with an ivory image of Christ, and a light hanging before it in a pierced metal ball suspended by three chains. The principal seat, placed towards the other side of the room and opposite the window, is a Turkish ottoman. The counterpane and hangings of the bed, the window curtains, the little carpet, and all the ornamental textile fabrics in the room are oriental and gorgeous: the paper on the walls is occidental and paltry. The washstand, against the wall on the side nearest the ottoman and window, consists of an enamelled iron basin with a pail beneath it in a painted metal frame, and a single towel on the rail at the side. The dressing table, between the bed and the window, is a common pine table, covered with a cloth of many colors, with an expensive toilet mirror on it. The door is on the side nearest the bed; and there is a chest of drawers between. This chest of drawers is also covered by a variegated native cloth; and on it there is a pile of paper backed novels, a box of chocolate creams, and a miniature easel with a large photograph of an extremely handsome officer, whose lofty bearing and magnetic glance can be felt even from the portrait. The room is lighted by a candle on the chest of drawers, and another on the dressing table with a box of matches beside it.

The window is hinged doorwise and stands wide open. Outside, a pair of wooden shutters, opening outwards, also stand open. On the balcony a young lady, intensely conscious of the romantic beauty of the night, and of the fact that her own youth and beauty are part of it, is gazing at the snowy Balkans. She is in her nightgown, well covered by a long mantle of furs, worth, on a moderate estimate, about three times the furniture of her room.

Her reverie is interrupted by her mother, Catherine Petkoff, a woman over forty, imperiously energetic, with magnificent black hair and eyes, who might be a very splendid specimen of the wife of a mountain farmer, but is determined to be a Viennese lady, and to that end wears a fashionable tea gown on all occasions.

CATHERINE [*entering hastily, full of good news*] Raina! [*She pronounces it Rah-eena, with the stress on the ee*]. Raina! [*She goes to the bed, expecting to find Raina there*]. Why, where—? [*Raina looks into the room*]. Heavens, child! are you out in the night air instead of in your bed? You'll catch your death. Louka told me you were asleep.

RAINA [*dreamily*] I sent her away. I wanted to be alone. The stars are so beautiful! What is the matter?

CATHERINE. Such news! There has been a battle.

RAINA [*her eyes dilating*] Ah! [*She comes eagerly to Catherine*].

CATHERINE. A great battle at Slivnitza! A victory! And it was won by Sergius.

RAINA [*with a cry of delight*] Ah! [*They embrace rapturously*] Oh, mother! [*Then, with sudden anxiety*] Is father safe?

CATHERINE. Of course: he sends me the news. Sergius is the hero of the hour, the idol of the regiment.

RAINA. Tell me, tell me. How was it? [*Ecstatically*] Oh, mother! mother! mother! [*She pulls her mother down on the ottoman; and they kiss one another frantically*].

CATHERINE [*with surging enthusiasm*] You cant guess how splendid it is. A cavalry charge! think of that! He defied our Russian commanders—acted without orders—led a charge on his own responsibility—headed it himself—was the first man to sweep through their guns. Cant you see it, Raina: our gallant splendid Bulgarians with their swords and eyes flashing, thundering down like an avalanche and scattering the wretched Serbs and their dandified Austrian officers like chaff. And you! you kept Sergius waiting a year before you would be betrothed to him. Oh, if you have a drop of Bulgarian blood in your veins, you will worship him when he comes back.

RAINA. What will he care for my poor little worship after the acclamations of a whole army of heroes? But no matter: I am so happy! so proud! [*She rises and walks about excitedly*]. It proves that all our ideas were real after all.

CATHERINE [*indignantly*] Our ideas real! What do you mean?

RAINA. Our ideas of what Sergius would do. Our patriotism. Our heroic ideals. I sometimes used to doubt whether they were anything but dreams. Oh, what faithless little creatures girls are! When I buckled on Sergius's sword he looked so noble: it was treason to think of disillusion or humiliation or failure. And yet —and yet—[*She sits down again suddenly*] Promise me youll never tell him.

CATHERINE. Dont ask me for promises until I know what I'm promising.

RAINA. Well, it came into my head just as he was holding me in his arms and looking into my eyes, that perhaps we only had our heroic ideas because we are so fond of reading Byron and Pushkin, and because we were so delighted with the opera that season at Bucharest. Real life is so seldom like that! indeed never, as far as I knew it then. [*Remorsefully*] Only think, mother: I doubted him: I wondered whether all his heroic qualities and his soldiership might not prove mere imagination when he went into a real battle. I had an uneasy fear that he might cut a poor figure there beside all those clever officers from the Tsar's court.

CATHERINE. A poor figure! Shame on you! The Serbs have Austrian officers who are just as clever as the Russians; but we have beaten them in every battle for all that.

RAINA [*laughing and snuggling against her mother*] Yes: I was only a prosaic little coward. Oh, to think that it was all true! that Sergius is just as splendid and noble as he looks! that the world is really a glorious world for women who can see its glory and men who can act its romance! What happiness! what unspeakable fulfilment!

They are interrupted by the entry of Louka, a handsome proud girl in a pretty Bulgarian peasant's dress with double apron, so defiant that her servility to Raina is almost insolent. She is afraid of Catherine, but even with her goes as far as she dares.

LOUKA. If you please, madam, all the windows are to be closed and the shutters made fast. They say there may be shooting in the streets. [*Raina and Catherine rise together, alarmed*]. The Serbs are being chased right back through the pass; and they say they may run into the town. Our cavalry will be after them; and our people will be ready for them, you may be sure, now theyre running away. [*She goes out on the balcony, and pulls the outside shutters to; then steps back into the room*].

CATHERINE [*businesslike, her housekeeping instincts aroused*] I must see that everything is made safe downstairs.

RAINA. I wish our people were not so cruel. What glory is there in killing wretched fugitives?

CATHERINE. Cruel! Do you suppose they would hesitate to kill you—or worse?

RAINA [*to Louka*] Leave the shutters so that I can just close them if I hear any noise.

CATHERINE [*authoritatively, turning on her way to the door*] Oh no, dear: you must keep them fastened. You would be sure to drop off to sleep and leave them open. Make them fast, Louka.

LOUKA. Yes, madam. [*She fastens them*].

RAINA. Dont be anxious about me. The moment I hear a shot, I shall blow out the candles and roll myself up in bed with my ears well covered.

CATHERINE. Quite the wisest thing you can do, my love. Goodnight.

RAINA. Goodnight. [*Her emotion comes back for a moment*]. Wish me joy [*They kiss*]. This is the happiest night of my life—if only there are no fugitives.

CATHERINE. Go to bed, dear; and dont think of them. [*She goes out*].

LOUKA [*secretly, to Raina*] If you would like the shutters open, just give them a push like this [*she pushes them: they open: she pulls them to again*]. One of them ought to be bolted at the bottom; but the bolt's gone.

RAINA [*with dignity, reproving her*] Thanks, Louka; but we must do what we are told. [*Louka makes a grimace*]. Goodnight.

LOUKA [*carelessly*] Goodnight. [*She goes out, swaggering*].

Raina, left alone, takes off her fur cloak and throws it on the ottoman. Then she goes to the chest of drawers, and adores the portrait there with feelings that are beyond all expression. She does not kiss it or press it to her breast, or shew it any mark of bodily affection; but she takes it in her hands and elevates it, like a priestess.

RAINA [*looking up at the picture*] Oh, I shall never be unworthy of you any more, my soul's hero: never, never, never. [*She replaces it reverently. Then she selects a novel from the little pile of books. She turns over the leaves dreamily; finds her page; turns the book inside out at it, and, with a happy sigh, gets into bed and prepares to read herself to sleep. But before abandoning herself to fiction, she raises her eyes once more, thinking of the blessed reality, and murmurs*] My hero! my hero!

A distant shot breaks the quiet of the night. She starts, listening; and two more shots, much nearer, follow, startling her so that she scrambles out of bed, and hastily blows out the candle on the chest of drawers. Then, putting her fingers in her ears, she runs to the dressing table, blows out the light there, and hurries back to bed in the dark, nothing being visible but the glimmer of the light in the pierced ball before the image, and the starlight seen through the slits at the top of the shutters. The firing breaks out again: there is a startling fusillade quite close at hand. Whilst it is still echoing, the shutters disappear, pulled open from without; and for an instant the rectangle of snowy starlight flashes out with the figure of a man silhouetted in black upon it. The shutters close immediately; and the room is dark again. But the silence is now broken by the sound of panting. Then

*there is a scratch; and the flame of a match is seen in the middle of
the room.*

RAINA [*crouching on the bed*] Who's there? [*The match is out
instantly*]. Who's there? Who is that?

A MAN'S VOICE [*in the darkness, subduedly, but threateningly*]
Sh—sh! Dont call out; or youll be shot. Be good; and no harm
will happen to you. [*She is heard leaving her bed, and making for
the door*]. Take care: it's no use trying to run away.

RAINA. But who—

THE VOICE [*warning*] Remember: if you raise your voice my
revolver will go off. [*Commandingly*] Strike a light and let me see
you. Do you hear. [*Another moment of silence and darkness as she
retreats to the chest of drawers. Then she lights a candle; and the
mystery is at an end. He is a man of about 35, in a deplorable plight,
bespattered with mud and blood and snow, his belt and the strap of
his revolver-case keeping together the torn ruins of the blue tunic
of a Serbian artillery officer. All that the candlelight and his un-
washed unkempt condition make it possible to discern is that he is of
middling stature and undistinguished appearance, with strong neck and
shoulders, roundish obstinate looking head covered with short crisp
bronze curls, clear quick eyes and good brows and mouth, hopelessly
prosaic nose like that of a strong minded baby, trim soldierlike
carriage and energetic manner; and with all his wits about him in
spite of his desperate predicament: even with a sense of the humor of
it, without, however, the least intention of trifling with it or throwing
away a chance. Reckoning up what he can guess about Raina: her age,
her social position, her character, and the extent to which she is
frightened, he continues, more politely but still most determinedly*]
Excuse my disturbing you; but you recognize my uniform? Serb!
If I'm caught I shall be killed. [*Menacingly*] Do you understand
that?

RAINA. Yes.

THE MAN. Well, I dont intend to get killed if I can help it. [*Still
more formidably*] Do you understand that? [*He locks the door
quickly but quietly*].

RAINA [*disdainfully*] I suppose not. [*She draws herself up superbly, and looks him straight in the face, adding, with cutting emphasis*] S o m e soldiers, I know, are afraid to die.

THE MAN [*with grim goodhumor*] All of them, dear lady, all of them, believe me. It is our duty to live as long as we can. Now, if you raise an alarm—

RAINA [*cutting him short*] You will shoot me. How do you know that *I* am afraid to die?

THE MAN [*cunningly*] Ah; but suppose I dont shoot you, what will happen then? A lot of your cavalry will burst into this pretty room of yours and slaughter me here like a pig; for I'll fight like a demon: they shant get m e into the street to amuse themselves with: I know what they are. Are you prepared to receive that sort of company in your present undress? [*Raina, suddenly conscious of her nightgown, instinctively shrinks, and gathers it more closely about her neck. He watches her, and adds, pitilessly*] Hardly presentable, eh? [*She turns to the ottoman. He raises his pistol instantly, and cries*] Stop! [*She stops*]. Where are you going?

RAINA [*with dignified patience*] Only to get my cloak.

THE MAN [*passing swiftly to the ottoman and snatching the cloak*] A good idea! I'll keep the cloak; and youll take care that nobody comes in and sees you without it. This is a better weapon than the revolver: eh? [*He throws the pistol down on the ottoman*].

RAINA [*revolted*] It is not the weapon of a gentleman!

THE MAN. It's good enough for a man with only you to stand between him and death. [*As they look at one another for a moment, Raina hardly able to believe that even a Serbian officer can be so cynically and selfishly unchivalrous, they are startled by a sharp fusillade in the street. The chill of imminent death hushes the man's voice as he adds*] Do you hear? If you are going to bring those blackguards in on me you shall receive them as you are.

Clamor and disturbance. The pursuers in the street batter at the house door, shouting Open the door! Open the door! Wake up, will you! *A man servant's voice calls to them angrily from within* This is Major Petkoff's house: you cant come in here; *but a*

*renewal of the clamor, and a torrent of blows on the door, end with
his letting a chain down with a clank, followed by a rush of heavy
footsteps and a din of triumphant yells, dominated at last by the
voice of Catherine, indignantly addressing an officer with* What does
this mean, sir? Do you know where you are? *The noise subsides
suddenly.*

LOUKA [*outside, knocking at the bedroom door*] My lady! my
lady! get up quick and open the door. If you dont they will break
it down.

*The fugitive throws up his head with the gesture of a man who
sees that it is all over with him, and drops the manner he has been
assuming to intimidate Raina.*

THE MAN [*sincerely and kindly*] No use, dear: I'm done for.
[*Flinging the cloak to her*] Quick! wrap yourself up: theyre coming.

RAINA. Oh, thank you. [*She wraps herself up with intense relief*].

THE MAN [*between his teeth*] Dont mention it.

RAINA [*anxiously*] What will you do?

THE MAN [*grimly*] The first man in will find out. Keep out of
the way; and dont look. It wont last long; but it will not be nice.
[*He draws his sabre and faces the door, waiting*].

RAINA [*impulsively*] I'll help you. I'll save you.

THE MAN. You cant.

RAINA. I can. I'll hide you. [*She drags him towards the window*].
Here! behind the curtains.

THE MAN [*yielding to her*] Theres just half a chance, if you keep
your head.

RAINA [*drawing the curtain before him*] S-sh! [*She makes for the
ottoman*].

THE MAN [*putting out his head*] Remember—

RAINA [*running back to him*] Yes?

THE MAN.—nine soldiers out of ten are born fools.

RAINA. Oh! [*She draws the curtain angrily before him*].

THE MAN [*looking out at the other side*] If they find me, I promise
you a fight: a devil of a fight.

She stamps at him. He disappears hastily. She takes off her cloak, and throws it across the foot of the bed. Then, with a sleepy, disturbed air, she opens the door. Louka enters excitedly.

LOUKA. One of those beasts of Serbs has been seen climbing up the waterpipe to your balcony. Our men want to search for him; and they are so wild and drunk and furious. [*She makes for the other side of the room to get as far from the door as possible*]. My lady says you are to dress at once, and to—[*She sees the revolver lying on the ottoman, and stops, petrified*].

RAINA [*as if annoyed at being disturbed*] They shall not search here. Why have they been let in?

CATHERINE [*coming in hastily*] Raina, darling: are you safe? Have you seen anyone or heard anything?

RAINA. I heard the shooting. Surely the soldiers will not dare come in here?

CATHERINE. I have found a Russian officer, thank Heaven: he knows Sergius. [*Speaking through the door to someone outside*] Sir: will you come in now. My daughter will receive you.

A young Russian officer, in Bulgarian uniform, enters, sword in hand.

OFFICER [*with soft feline politeness and stiff military carriage*] Good evening, gracious lady. I am sorry to intrude; but there is a Serb hiding on the balcony. Will you and the gracious lady your mother please to withdraw whilst we search?

RAINA [*petulantly*] Nonsense, sir: you can see that there is no one on the balcony. [*She throws the shutters wide open and stands with her back to the curtain where the man is hidden, pointing to the moonlit balcony. A couple of shots are fired right under the window; and a bullet shatters the glass opposite Raina, who winks and gasps, but stands her ground; whilst Catherine screams, and the officer, with a cry of Take care! rushes to the balcony*].

THE OFFICER [*on the balcony, shouting savagely down to the street*] Cease firing there, you fools: do you hear? Cease firing, damn you! [*He glares down for a moment; then turns to Raina, trying to resume his polite manner*]. Could anyone have got in without your knowledge? Were you asleep?

RAINA. No: I have not been to bed.

THE OFFICER [*impatiently, coming back into the room*] Your neighbors have their heads so full of runaway Serbs that they see them everywhere. [*Politely*] Gracious lady: a thousand pardons. Goodnight. [*Military bow, which Raina returns coldly. Another to Catherine, who follows him out*].

Raina closes the shutters. She turns and sees Louka, who has been watching the scene curiously.

RAINA. Dont leave my mother, Louka, until the soldiers go away.

Louka glances at Raina, at the ottoman, at the curtain; then purses her lips secretively, laughs insolently, and goes out. Raina, highly offended by this demonstration, follows her to the door, and shuts it behind her with a slam, locking it violently. The man immediately steps out from behind the curtain, sheathing his sabre. Then, dismissing the danger from his mind in a businesslike way, he comes affably to Raina.

THE MAN. A narrow shave; but a miss is as good as a mile. Dear young lady: your servant to the death. I wish for your sake I had joined the Bulgarian army instead of the other one. I am not a native Serb.

RAINA [*haughtily*] No: you are one of the Austrians who set the Serbs on to rob us of our national liberty, and who officer their army for them. We hate them!

THE MAN. Austrian! not I. Dont hate me, dear young lady. I am a Swiss, fighting merely as a professional soldier. I joined the Serbs because they came first on the road from Switzerland. Be generous: youve beaten us hollow.

RAINA. Have I not been generous?

THE MAN. Noble! Heroic! But I'm not saved yet. This particular rush will soon pass through; but the pursuit will go on all night by fits and starts. I must take my chance to get off in a quiet interval. [*Pleasantly*] You dont mind my waiting just a minute or two, do you?

RAINA [*putting on her most genteel society manner*] Oh, not at all. Wont you sit down?

THE MAN. Thanks. [*He sits on the foot of the bed*].

Raina walks with studied elegance to the ottoman and sits down. Unfortunately she sits on the pistol, and jumps up with a shriek. The man, all nerves, shies like a frightened horse to the other side of the room.

THE MAN [*irritably*] Dont frighten me like that. What is it?

RAINA. Your revolver! It was staring that officer in the face all the time. What an escape!

THE MAN [*vexed at being unnecessarily terrified*] Oh, is that all?

RAINA [*staring at him rather superciliously as she conceives a poorer and poorer opinion of him, and feels proportionately more and more at her ease*] I am sorry I frightened you. [*She takes up the pistol and hands it to him*]. Pray take it to protect yourself against me.

THE MAN [*grinning wearily at the sarcasm as he takes the pistol*] No use, dear young lady: theres nothing in it. It's not loaded. [*He makes a grimace at it, and drops it disparagingly into his revolver case*].

RAINA. Load it by all means.

THE MAN. Ive no ammunition. What use are cartridges in battle? I always carry chocolate instead; and I finished the last cake of that hours ago.

RAINA [*outraged in her most cherished ideals of manhood*] Chocolate! Do you stuff your pockets with sweets—like a schoolboy —even in the field?

THE MAN [*grinning*] Yes: isnt it contemptible? [*Hungrily*] I wish I had some now.

RAINA. Allow me. [*She sails away scornfully to the chest of drawers, and returns with the box of confectionery in her hand*]. I am sorry I have eaten them all except these. [*She offers him the box*].

THE MAN [*ravenously*] Youre an angel! [*He gobbles the contents*]. Creams! Delicious! [*He looks anxiously to see whether there are any more. There are none: he can only scrape the box with his fingers and suck them. When that nourishment is exhausted he accepts the*

C

inevitable with pathetic goodhumor, and says, with grateful emotion]
Bless you, dear lady! You can always tell an old soldier by the
inside of his holsters and cartridge boxes. The young ones carry
pistols and cartridges: the old ones, grub. Thank you. [*He hands
back the box. She snatches it contemptuously from him and throws it
away. He shies again, as if she had meant to strike him*]. Ugh! Dont
do things so suddenly, gracious lady. It's mean to revenge yourself because I frightened you just now.

RAINA [*loftily*] Frighten me! Do you know, sir, that though I
am only a woman, I think I am at heart as brave as you.

THE MAN. I should think so. You havnt been under fire for three
days as I have. I can stand two days without shewing it much; but
no man can stand three days: I'm as nervous as a mouse. [*He sits
down on the ottoman, and takes his head in his hands*]. Would you
like to see me cry?

RAINA [*alarmed*] No.

THE MAN. If you would, all you have to do is to scold me just
as if I were a little boy and you my nurse. If I were in camp now,
theyd play all sorts of tricks on me.

RAINA [*a little moved*] I'm sorry. I wont scold you. [*Touched by
the sympathy in her tone, he raises his head and looks gratefully at
her: she immediately draws back and says stiffly*] You must excuse
me: our soldiers are not like that. [*She moves away from the
ottoman*].

THE MAN. Oh yes they are. There are only two sorts of soldiers:
old ones and young ones. Ive served fourteen years: half of your
fellows never smelt powder before. Why, how is it that youve
just beaten us? Sheer ignorance of the art of war, nothing else.
[*Indignantly*] I never saw anything so unprofessional.

RAINA [*ironically*] Oh! was it unprofessional to beat you?

THE MAN. Well, come! is it professional to throw a regiment of
cavalry on a battery of machine guns, with the dead certainty that
if the guns go off not a horse or man will ever get within fifty
yards of the fire? I couldnt believe my eyes when I saw it.

RAINA [*eagerly turning to him, as all her enthusiasm and her dreams of glory rush back on her*] Did you see the great cavalry charge? Oh, tell me about it. Describe it to me.

THE MAN. You never saw a cavalry charge, did you?

RAINA. How could I?

THE MAN. Ah, perhaps not. No: of course not! Well, it's a funny sight. It's like slinging a handful of peas against a window pane: first one comes; then two or three close behind him; and then all the rest in a lump.

RAINA [*her eyes dilating as she raises her clasped hands ecstatically*] Yes, first One! the bravest of the brave!

THE MAN [*prosaically*] Hm! you should see the poor devil pulling at his horse.

RAINA. Why should he pull at his horse?

THE MAN [*impatient of so stupid a question*] It's running away with him, of course: do you suppose the fellow wants to get there before the others and be killed? Then they all come. You can tell the young ones by their wildness and their slashing. The old ones come bunched up under the number one guard: they know that theyre mere projectiles, and that it's no use trying to fight. The wounds are mostly broken knees, from the horses cannoning together.

RAINA. Ugh! But I dont believe the first man is a coward. I know he is a hero!

THE MAN [*goodhumoredly*] Thats what youd have said if youd seen the first man in the charge today.

RAINA [*breathless, forgiving him everything*] Ah, I knew it! Tell me. Tell me about him.

THE MAN. He did it like an operatic tenor. A regular handsome fellow, with flashing eyes and lovely moustache, shouting his war-cry and charging like Don Quixote at the windmills. We did laugh.

RAINA. You dared to laugh!

THE MAN. Yes; but when the sergeant ran up as white as a sheet, and told us theyd sent us the wrong ammunition, and that we couldnt fire a round for the next ten minutes, we laughed at the other side of our mouths. I never felt so sick in my life; though Ive been in one or two very tight places. And I hadnt even a revolver cartridge: only chocolate. We'd no bayonets: nothing. Of course, they just cut us to bits. And there was Don Quixote flourishing like a drum major, thinking he'd done the cleverest thing ever known, whereas he ought to be courtmartialled for it. Of all the fools ever let loose on a field of battle, that man must be the very maddest. He and his regiment simply committed suicide; only the pistol missed fire: thats all.

RAINA [*deeply wounded, but steadfastly loyal to her ideals*] Indeed! Would you know him again if you saw him?

THE MAN. Shall I ever forget him!

She again goes to the chest of drawers. He watches her with a vague hope that she may have something more for him to eat. She takes the portrait from its stand and brings it to him.

RAINA. That is a photograph of the gentleman—the patriot and hero—to whom I am betrothed.

THE MAN [*recognizing it with a shock*] I'm really very sorry. [*Looking at her*] Was it fair to lead me on? [*He looks at the portrait again*] Yes: thats Don Quixote: not a doubt of it. [*He stifles a laugh*].

RAINA [*quickly*] Why do you laugh?

THE MAN [*apologetic, but still greatly tickled*] I didnt laugh, I assure you. At least I didnt mean to. But when I think of him charging the windmills and imagining he was doing the finest thing—[*He chokes with suppressed laughter*].

RAINA [*sternly*] Give me back the portrait, sir.

THE MAN [*with sincere remorse*] Of course. Certainly. I'm really very sorry. [*He hands her the picture. She deliberately kisses it and looks him straight in the face before returning to the chest of drawers to replace it. He follows her, apologizing*]. Perhaps I'm quite wrong, you know: no doubt I am. Most likely he had got wind of the cartridge business somehow, and knew it was a safe job.

RAINA. That is to say, he was a pretender and a coward! You did not dare say that before.

THE MAN [*with a comic gesture of despair*] It's no use, dear lady: I cant make you see it from the professional point of view. [*As he turns away to get back to the ottoman, a couple of distant shots threaten renewed trouble*].

RAINA [*sternly, as she sees him listening to the shots*] So much the better for you!

THE MAN [*turning*] How?

RAINA. You are my enemy; and you are at my mercy. What would I do if I were a professional soldier?

THE MAN. Ah, true, dear young lady: youre always right. I know how good youve been to me: to my last hour I shall remember those three chocolate creams. It was unsoldierly; but it was angelic.

RAINA [*coldly*] Thank you. And now I will do a soldierly thing. You cannot stay here after what you have just said about my future husband; but I will go out on the balcony and see whether it is safe for you to climb down into the street. [*She turns to the window*].

THE MAN [*changing countenance*] Down that waterpipe! Stop! Wait! I cant! I darent! The very thought of it makes me giddy. I came up it fast enough with death behind me. But to face it now in cold blood—! [*He sinks on the ottoman*]. It's no use: I give up: I'm beaten. Give the alarm. [*He drops his head on his hands in the deepest dejection*].

RAINA [*disarmed by pity*] Come: dont be disheartened. [*She stoops over him almost maternally; he shakes his head*]. Oh, you are a very poor soldier: a chocolate cream soldier! Come, cheer up! it takes less courage to climb down than to face capture: remember that.

THE MAN [*dreamily, lulled by her voice*] No: capture only means death; and death is sleep: oh, sleep, sleep, sleep, undisturbed sleep! Climbing down the pipe means doing something—exerting myself—thinking! Death ten times over first.

RAINA [*softly and wonderingly, catching the rhythm of his weariness*] Are you as sleepy as that?

THE MAN. Ive not had two hours undisturbed sleep since I joined. I havnt closed my eyes for forty-eight hours.

RAINA [*at her wit's end*] But what am I to do with you?

THE MAN [*staggering up, roused by her desperation*] Of course. I must do something. [*He shakes himself; pulls himself together; and speaks with rallied vigor and courage*]. You see, sleep or no sleep, hunger or no hunger, tired or not tired, you can always do a thing when you know it must be done. Well, that pipe must be got down: [*he hits himself on the chest*] do you hear that, you chocolate cream soldier? [*He turns to the window*].

RAINA [*anxiously*] But if you fall?

THE MAN. I shall sleep as if the stones were a feather bed. Goodbye. [*He makes boldly for the window; and his hand is on the shutter when there is a terrible burst of firing in the street beneath*].

RAINA [*rushing to him*] Stop! [*She seizes him recklessly, and pulls him quite round*]. Theyll kill you.

THE MAN [*coolly, but attentively*] Never mind: this sort of thing is all in my day's work. I'm bound to take my chance. [*Decisively*] Now do what I tell you. Put out the candle; so that they shant see the light when I open the shutters. And keep away from the window, whatever you do. If they see me theyre sure to have a shot at me.

RAINA [*clinging to him*] Theyre sure to see you: it's bright moonlight. I'll save you. Oh, how can you be so indifferent! You want me to save you, dont you?

THE MAN. I really dont want to be troublesome. [*She shakes him in her impatience*]. I am not indifferent, dear young lady, I assure you. But how is it to be done?

RAINA. Come away from the window. [*She takes him firmly back to the middle of the room. The moment she releases him he turns mechanically towards the window again. She seizes him and turns him back, exclaiming*] Please! [*He becomes motionless, like a hypnotized rabbit, his fatigue gaining fast on him. She releases him, and addresses him patronizingly*]. Now listen. You must trust to our h ospitality. You do not yet know in whose house you are. I am a Petkoff.

THE MAN. A pet what?

RAINA [*rather indignantly*] I mean that I belong to the family of the Petkoffs, the richest and best known in our country.

THE MAN. Oh yes, of course. I beg your pardon. The Petkoffs, to be sure. How stupid of me!

RAINA. You know you never heard of them until this moment. How can you stoop to pretend!

THE MAN. Forgive me: I'm too tired to think; and the change of subject was too much for me. Dont scold me.

RAINA. I forgot. It might make you cry. [*He nods, quite seriously. She pouts and then resumes her patronizing tone*]. I must tell you that my father holds the highest command of any Bulgarian in our army. He is [*proudly*] a Major.

THE MAN [*pretending to be deeply impressed*] A Major! Bless me! Think of that!

RAINA. You shewed great ignorance in thinking that it was necessary to climb up to the balcony because ours is the only private house that has two rows of windows. There is a flight of stairs inside to get up and down by.

THE MAN. Stairs! How grand! You live in great luxury indeed, dear young lady.

RAINA. Do you know what a library is?

THE MAN. A library? A roomful of books?

RAINA. Yes. We have one, the only one in Bulgaria.

THE MAN. Actually a real library! I should like to see that.

RAINA [*affectedly*] I tell you these things to shew you that you are not in the house of ignorant country folk who would kill you the moment they saw your Serbian uniform, but among civilized people. We go to Bucharest every year for the opera season; and I have spent a whole month in Vienna.

THE MAN. I saw that, dear young lady. I saw at once that you knew the world.

RAINA. Have you ever seen the opera of Ernani?

THE MAN. Is that the one with the devil in it in red velvet, and a soldiers' chorus?

RAINA [*contemptuously*] No!

THE MAN [*stifling a heavy sigh of weariness*] Then I dont know it.

RAINA. I thought you might have remembered the great scene where Ernani, flying from his foes just as you are tonight, takes refuge in the castle of his bitterest enemy, an old Castilian noble. The noble refuses to give him up. His guest is sacred to him.

THE MAN [*quickly, waking up a little*] Have your people got that notion?

RAINA [*with dignity*] My mother and I can understand that notion, as you call it. And if instead of threatening me with your pistol as you did you had simply thrown yourself as a fugitive on our hospitality, you would have been as safe as in your father's house.

THE MAN. Quite sure?

RAINA [*turning her back on him in disgust*] Oh, it is useless to try to make you understand.

THE MAN. Dont be angry: you see how awkward it would be for me if there was any mistake. My father is a very hospitable man: he keeps six hotels; but I couldnt trust him as far as that. What about your father?

RAINA. He is away at Slivnitza fighting for his country. I answer for your safety. There is my hand in pledge of it. Will that reassure you? [*She offers him her hand*].

THE MAN [*looking dubiously at his own hand*] Better not touch my hand, dear young lady. I must have a wash first.

RAINA [*touched*] That is very nice of you. I see that you are a gentleman.

THE MAN [*puzzled*] Eh?

RAINA. You must not think I am surprised. Bulgarians of really good standing—people in our position—wash their hands nearly every day. So you see I can appreciate your delicacy. You may take my hand. [*She offers it again*].

THE MAN [*kissing it with his hands behind his back*] Thanks, gracious young lady: I feel safe at last. And now would you mind breaking the news to your mother? I had better not stay here secretly longer than is necessary.

RAINA. If you will be so good as to keep perfectly still whilst I am away.

THE MAN. Certainly. [*He sits down on the ottoman*].

Raina goes to the bed and wraps herself in the fur cloak. His eyes close. She goes to the door. Turning for a last look at him, she sees that he is dropping off to sleep.

RAINA [*at the door*] You are not going asleep, are you? [*He murmurs inarticulately: she runs to him and shakes him*]. Do you hear? Wake up: you are falling asleep.

THE MAN. Eh? Falling aslee—? Oh no: not the least in the world: I was only thinking. It's all right: I'm wide awake.

RAINA [*severely*] Will you please stand up while I am away. [*He rises reluctantly*]. All the time, mind.

THE MAN [*standing unsteadily*] Certainly. Certainly: you may depend on me.

Raina looks doubtfully at him. He smiles weakly. She goes reluctantly, turning again at the door, and almost catching him in the act of yawning. She goes out.

THE MAN [*drowsily*] Sleep, sleep, sleep, sleep, slee—[*The words trail off into a murmur. He wakes again with a shock on the point of falling*]. Where am I? Thats what I want to know: where am I? Must keep awake. Nothing keeps me awake except danger: remember that: [*intently*] danger, danger, danger, dan—[*trailing off again: another shock*] Wheres danger? Mus' find it. [*He starts off vaguely round the room in search of it*]. What am I looking for? Sleep—danger—dont know. [*He stumbles against the bed*]. Ah yes: now I know. All right now. I'm to go to bed, but not to sleep. Be sure not to sleep, because of danger. Not to lie down either, only sit down. [*He sits on the bed. A blissful expression comes into his face*]. Ah! [*With a happy sigh he sinks back at full length; lifts his boots into the bed with a final effort; and falls fast asleep instantly*].

Catherine comes in, followed by Raina.

RAINA [*looking at the ottoman*] He's gone! I left him here.

CATHERINE. Here! Then he must have climbed down from the—

RAINA [*seeing him*] Oh! [*She points*].

CATHERINE [*scandalized*] Well! [*She strides to the bed, Raina following until she is opposite her on the other side*]. He's fast asleep. The brute!

RAINA [*anxiously*] Sh!

CATHERINE [*shaking him*] Sir! [*Shaking him again, harder*] Sir!! [*Vehemently, shaking very hard*] Sir!!!

RAINA [*catching her arm*] Dont, mamma: the poor darling is worn out. Let him sleep.

CATHERINE [*letting him go, and turning amazed to Raina*] The poor darling! Raina!!! [*She looks sternly at her daughter*].

The man sleeps profoundly.

ACT II

The sixth of March, 1886. In the garden of Major Petkoff's house. It is a fine spring morning: the garden looks fresh and pretty. Beyond the paling the tops of a couple of minarets can be seen, shewing that there is a valley there, with the little town in it. A few miles further the Balkan mountains rise and shut in the landscape. Looking towards them from within the garden, the side of the house is seen on the left, with a garden door reached by a little flight of steps. On the right the stable yard, with its gateway, encroaches on the garden. There are fruit bushes along the paling and house, covered with washing spread out to dry. A path runs by the house, and rises by two steps at the corner, where it turns out of sight. In the middle, a small table, with two bent wood chairs at it, is laid for breakfast with Turkish coffee pot, cups, rolls, etc.; but the cups have been used and the bread broken. There is a wooden garden seat against the wall on the right.

Louka, smoking a cigaret, is standing between the table and the house, turning her back with angry disdain on a man servant who is lecturing her. He is a middle-aged man of cool temperament and low but clear and keen intelligence, with the complacency of the servant who values himself on his rank in servitude, and the imperturbability of the accurate calculator who has no illusions. He wears a white Bulgarian costume: jacket with embroidered border, sash, wide knickerbockers, and decorated gaiters. His head is shaved up to the crown, giving him a high Japanese forehead. His name is Nicola.

NICOLA. Be warned in time, Louka: mend your manners. I know the mistress. She is so grand that she never dreams that any servant could dare be disrespectful to her, but if she once suspects that you are defying her, out you go.

LOUKA. I do defy her. I will defy her. What do I care for her?

NICOLA. If you quarrel with the family, I never can marry you. It's the same as if you quarrelled with me!

LOUKA. You take her part against me, do you?

NICOLA [*sedately*] I shall always be dependent on the good will of the family. When I leave their service and start a shop in Sofia, their custom will be half my capital: their bad word would ruin me.

LOUKA. You have no spirit. I should like to catch them saying a word against me!

NICOLA [*pityingly*] I should have expected more sense from you, Louka. But youre young: youre young!

LOUKA. Yes; and you like me the better for it, dont you? But I know some family secrets they wouldnt care to have told, young as I am. Let them quarrel with me if they dare!

NICOLA [*with compassionate superiority*] Do you know what they would do if they heard you talk like that?

LOUKA. What could they do?

NICOLA. Discharge you for untruthfulness. Who would believe any stories you told after that? Who would give you another situation? Who in this house would dare be seen speaking to you ever again? How long would your father be left on his little farm? [*She impatiently throws away the end of her cigaret, and stamps on it*]. Child: you dont know the power such high people have over the like of you and me when we try to rise out of our poverty against them. [*He goes close to her and lowers his voice*]. Look at me, ten years in their service. Do you think I know no secrets? I know things about the mistress that she wouldnt have the master know for a thousand levas. I know things about him that she wouldnt let him hear the last of for six months if I blabbed them to her. I know things about Raina that would break off her match with Sergius if—

LOUKA [*turning on him quickly*] How do you know? I never told you!

NICOLA [*opening his eyes cunningly*] So thats your little secret, is it? I thought it might be something like that. Well, you take my advice and be respectful; and make the mistress feel that no matter what you know or dont know, she can depend on you to hold your tongue and serve the family faithfully. Thats what they like; and thats how youll make most out of them.

LOUKA [*with searching scorn*] You have the soul of a servant, Nicola.

NICOLA [*complacently*] Yes: thats the secret of success in service.

A loud knocking with a whip handle on a wooden door is heard from the stable yard.

MALE VOICE OUTSIDE. Hollo! Hollo there! Nicola!

LOUKA. Master! back from the war!

NICOLA [*quickly*] My word for it, Louka, the war's over. Off with you and get some fresh coffee. [*He runs out into the stable yard*].

LOUKA [*as she collects the coffee pot and cups on the tray, and carries it into the house*] Youll never put the soul of a servant into me.

Major Petkoff comes from the stable yard, followed by Nicola. He is a cheerful, excitable, insignificant, unpolished man of about 50, naturally unambitious except as to his income and his importance in local society, but just now greatly pleased with the military rank which the war has thrust on him as a man of consequence in his town. The fear of plucky patriotism which the Serbian attack roused in all the Bulgarians has pulled him through the war; but he is obviously glad to be home again.

PETKOFF [*pointing to the table with his whip*] Breakfast out here, eh?

NICOLA. Yes, sir. The mistress and Miss Raina have just gone in.

PETKOFF [*sitting down and taking a roll*] Go in and say Ive come; and get me some fresh coffee.

NICOLA. It's coming, sir. [*He goes to the house door. Louka, with fresh coffee, a clean cup, and a brandy bottle on her tray, meets him*]. Have you told the mistress?

LOUKA. Yes: she's coming.

Nicola goes into the house. Louka brings the coffee to the table.

PETKOFF. Well: the Serbs havnt run away with you, have they?

LOUKA. No, sir.

PETKOFF. Thats right. Have you brought me some cognac?

LOUKA [*putting the bottle on the table*] Here, sir.

PETKOFF. Thats right. [*He pours some into his coffee*].

Catherine, who, having at this early hour made only a very perfunctory toilet, wears a Bulgarian apron over a once brilliant but now half worn-out dressing gown, and a colored handkerchief tied over her thick black hair, comes from the house with Turkish slippers on her bare feet, looking astonishingly handsome and stately under all the circumstances. Louka goes into the house.

CATHERINE. My dear Paul: what a surprise for us! [*She stoops over the back of his chair to kiss him*]. Have they brought you fresh coffee?

PETKOFF. Yes: Louka's been looking after me. The war's over. The treaty was signed three days ago at Bucharest; and the decree for our army to demobilize was issued yesterday.

CATHERINE [*springing erect, with flashing eyes*] Paul: have you let the Austrians force you to make peace?

PETKOFF [*submissively*] My dear: they didnt consult me. What could *I* do? [*She sits down and turns away from him*]. But of course we saw to it that the treaty was an honorable one. It declares peace—

CATHERINE [*outraged*] Peace!

PETKOFF [*appeasing her*]—but not friendly relations: remember that. They wanted to put that in; but I insisted on its being struck out. What more could I do?

CATHERINE. You could have annexed Serbia and made Prince Alexander Emperor of the Balkans. Thats what I would have done.

PETKOFF. I dont doubt it in the least, my dear. But I should have had to subdue the whole Austrian Empire first; and that would have kept me too long away from you. I missed you greatly.

CATHERINE [*relenting*] Ah! [*She stretches her hand affectionately across the table to squeeze his*].

PETKOFF. And how have you been, my dear?

CATHERINE. Oh, my usual sore throats: thats all.

PETKOFF [*with conviction*] That comes from washing your neck every day. Ive often told you so.

CATHERINE. Nonsense, Paul!

PETKOFF [*over his coffee and cigaret*] I dont believe in going too far with these modern customs. All this washing cant be good for the health: it's not natural. There was an Englishman at Philippopolis who used to wet himself all over with cold water every morning when he got up. Disgusting! It all comes from the English: their climate makes them so dirty that they have to be perpetually washing themselves. Look at my father! he never had a bath in his life; and he lived to be ninety-eight, the healthiest man in Bulgaria. I dont mind a good wash once a week to keep up my position; but once a day is carrying the thing to a ridiculous extreme.

CATHERINE. You are a barbarian at heart still, Paul. I hope you behaved yourself before all those Russian officers.

PETKOFF. I did my best. I took care to let them know that we have a library.

CATHERINE. Ah; but you didnt tell them that we have an electric bell in it? I have had one put up.

PETKOFF. Whats an electric bell?

CATHERINE. You touch a button; something tinkles in the kitchen; and then Nicola comes up.

PETKOFF. Why not shout for him?

CATHERINE. Civilized people never shout for their servants. Ive learnt that while you were away.

PETKOFF. Well, I'll tell you something Ive learnt too. Civilized people dont hang out their washing to dry where visitors can see it; so youd better have all that [*indicating the clothes on the bushes*] put somewhere else.

CATHERINE. Oh, thats absurd, Paul: I dont believe really refined people notice such things.

SERGIUS [*knocking at the stable gates*] Gate, Nicola!

PETKOFF. Theres Sergius. [*Shouting*] Hollo, Nicola!

CATHERINE. Oh, dont shout, Paul: it really isnt nice.

PETKOFF. Bosh! [*He shouts louder than before*] Nicola!

NICOLA [*appearing at the house door*] Yes, sir.

PETKOFF. Are you deaf? Dont you hear Major Saranoff knocking? Bring him round this way. [*He pronounces the name with the stress on the second syllable: Sarahnoff*].

NICOLA. Yes, major. [*He goes into the stable yard*].

PETKOFF. You must talk to him, my dear, until Raina takes him off our hands. He bores my life out about our not promoting him. Over my head, if you please.

CATHERINE. He certainly ought to be promoted when he marries Raina. Besides, the country should insist on having at least one native general.

PETKOFF. Yes; so that he could throw away whole brigades instead of regiments. It's no use, my dear: he hasnt the slightest chance of promotion until we're quite sure that the peace will be a lasting one.

NICOLA [*at the gate, announcing*] Major Sergius Saranoff! [*He goes into the house and returns presently with a third chair, which he places at the table. He then withdraws*].

Major Sergius Saranoff, the original of the portrait in Raina's room, is a tall romantically handsome man, with the physical hardihood, the high spirit, and the susceptible imagination of an untamed mountaineer chieftain. But his remarkable personal distinction is of a characteristically civilized type. The ridges of his eyebrows, curving with an interrogative twist round the projections at the outer corners; his jealously observant eye; his nose, thin, keen, and apprehensive in spite of the pugnacious high bridge and large nostril; his assertive chin, would not be out of place in a Parisian salon, shewing that the clever imaginative barbarian has an acute critical faculty which has been thrown into intense activity by the arrival of western civilization in the Balkans. The result is precisely what the advent of nineteenth century thought first produced in England: to wit, Byronism. By his brooding on the perpetual failure, not only of others, but of himself, to live up to his ideals; by his consequent cynical scorn for humanity; by his jejune credulity as to the absolute validity of his concepts and the unworthiness of the world in disregarding them; by his wincings and mockeries under the sting of the petty disillusions which every hour spent among men brings to his sensitive observation, he has acquired the half tragic, half ironic air, the mysterious moodiness, the suggestion of a strange and terrible history that has left nothing but undying remorse, by which Childe Harold fascinated the grandmothers of his English contemporaries. It is clear that here or nowhere is Raina's ideal hero. Catherine is hardly less enthusiastic about him than her daughter, and much less reserved in shewing her enthusiasm. As he enters from the stable gate, she rises effusively to greet him. Petkoff is distinctly less disposed to make a fuss about him.

PETKOFF. Here already, Sergius! Glad to see you.

CATHERINE. My dear Sergius! [*She holds out both her hands*].

SERGIUS [*kissing them with scrupulous gallantry*] My dear mother, if I may call you so.

PETKOFF [*drily*] Mother-in-law, Sergius: mother-in-law! Sit down; and have some coffee.

SERGIUS. Thank you: none for me. [*He gets away from the table with a certain distaste for Petkoff's enjoyment of it, and posts himself with conscious dignity against the rail of the steps leading to the house*].

CATHERINE. You look superb. The campaign has improved you, Sergius. Everybody here is mad about you. We were all wild with enthusiasm about that magnificent cavalry charge.

SERGIUS [*with grave irony*] Madam: it was the cradle and the grave of my military reputation.

CATHERINE. How so?

SERGIUS. I won the battle the wrong way when our worthy Russian generals were losing it the right way. In short, I upset their plans, and wounded their self-esteem. Two Cossack colonels had their regiments routed on the most correct principles of scientific warfare. Two major-generals got killed strictly according to military etiquette. The two colonels are now major-generals; and I am still a simple major.

CATHERINE. You shall not remain so, Sergius. The women are

D

on your side; and they will see that justice is done you.

SERGIUS. It is too late. I have only waited for the peace to send in my resignation.

PETKOFF [*dropping his cup in his amazement*] Your resignation!

CATHERINE. Oh, you must withdraw it!

SERGIUS [*with resolute measured emphasis, folding his arms*] I never withdraw.

PETKOFF [*vexed*] Now who could have supposed you were going to do such a thing?

SERGIUS [*with fire*] Everyone that knew me. But enough of myself and my affairs. How is Raina; and where is Raina?

RAINA [*suddenly coming round the corner of the house and standing at the top of the steps in the path*] Raina is here.

She makes a charming picture as they turn to look at her. She wears an underdress of pale green silk, draped with an overdress of thin ecru canvas embroidered with gold. She is crowned with a dainty eastern cap of gold tinsel. Sergius goes impulsively to meet her. Posing regally, she presents her hand: he drops chivalrously on one knee and kisses it.

PETKOFF [*aside to Catherine, beaming with parental pride*] Pretty, isnt it? She always appears at the right moment.

CATHERINE [*impatiently*] Yes: she listens for it. It is an abominable habit.

Sergius leads Raina forward with splendid gallantry. When they arrive at the table, she turns to him with a bend of the head: he bows; and thus they separate, he coming to his place, and she going behind her father's chair.

RAINA [*stooping and kissing her father*] Dear father! Welcome home!

PETKOFF [*patting her cheek*] My little pet girl. [*He kisses her. She goes to the chair left by Nicola for Sergius, and sits down*].

CATHERINE. And so youre no longer a soldier, Sergius.

SERGIUS. I am no longer a soldier. Soldiering, my dear madam, is the coward's art of attacking mercilessly when you are strong, and keeping out of harm's way when you are weak. That is the whole secret of successful fighting. Get your enemy at a disadvantage; and never, on any account, fight him on equal terms.

PETKOFF. They wouldnt let us make a fair stand-up fight of it. However, I suppose soldiering has to be a trade like any other trade.

SERGIUS. Precisely. But I have no ambition to shine as a tradesman; so I have taken the advice of that bagman of a captain that settled the exchange of prisoners with us at Pirot, and given it up.

PETKOFF. What! that Swiss fellow? Sergius: Ive often thought of that exchange since. He over-reached us about those horses.

SERGIUS. Of course he over-reached us. His father was a hotel and livery stable keeper; and he owed his first step to his knowledge of horse-dealing. [*With mock enthusiasm*] Ah, he was a soldier: every inch a soldier! If only I had bought the horses for my regiment instead of foolishly leading it into danger, I should have been a field-marshal now!

CATHERINE. A Swiss? What was he doing in the Serbian army?

PETKOFF. A volunteer, of course: keen on picking up his profession. [*Chuckling*] We shouldnt have been able to begin fighting if these foreigners hadnt shewn us how to do it: we knew nothing about it; and neither did the Serbs. Egad, there'd have been no war without them!

RAINA. Are there many Swiss officers in the Serbian army?

PETKOFF. No. All Austrians, just as our officers were all Russians. This was the only Swiss I came across. I'll never trust a Swiss again. He humbugged us into giving him fifty ablebodied men for two hundred worn out chargers. They werent even eatable!

SERGIUS. We were two children in the hands of that consummate soldier, Major: simply two innocent little children.

RAINA. What was he like?

CATHERINE. Oh, Raina, what a silly question!

SERGIUS. He was like a commercial traveller in uniform. Bourgeois to his boots!

PETKOFF [*grinning*] Sergius: tell Catherine that queer story his friend told us about how he escaped after Slivnitza. You remember. About his being hid by two women.

SERGIUS [*with bitter irony*] Oh yes: quite a romance! He was serving in the very battery I so unprofessionally charged. Being a thorough soldier, he ran away like the rest of them, with our cavalry at his heels. To escape their sabres he climbed a waterpipe and made his way into the bedroom of a young Bulgarian lady. The young lady was enchanted by his persuasive commercial traveller's manners. She very modestly entertained him for an hour or so, and then called in her mother lest her conduct should appear unmaidenly. The old lady was equally fascinated; and the fugitive was sent on his way in the morning, disguised in an old coat belonging to the master of the house, who was away at the war.

RAINA [*rising with marked stateliness*] Your life in the camp has made you coarse, Sergius. I did not think you would have repeated such a story before me. [*She turns away coldly*].

CATHERINE [*also rising*] She is right, Sergius. If such women exist, we should be spared the knowledge of them.

PETKOFF. Pooh! nonsense! what does it matter?

SERGIUS [*ashamed*] No, Petkoff: I was wrong. [*To Raina, with earnest humility*] I beg your pardon. I have behaved abominably. Forgive me, Raina. [*She bows reservedly*]. And you too, madam. [*Catherine bows graciously and sits down. He proceeds solemnly, again addressing Raina*] The glimpses I have had of the seamy side of life during the last few months have made me cynical; but I should not have brought my cynicism here: least of all into your presence, Raina. I—[*Here, turning to the others, he is evidently going to begin a long speech when the Major interrupts him*].

PETKOFF. Stuff and nonsense, Sergius! Thats quite enough fuss about nothing: a soldier's daughter should be able to stand up without flinching to a little strong conversation. [*He rises*]. Come: it's time for us to get to business. We have to make up our minds how those three regiments are to get back to Philippopolis: theres no forage for them on the Sofia route. [*He goes towards the house*].

Come along. [*Sergius is about to follow him when Catherine rises and intervenes*].

CATHERINE. Oh, Paul, cant you spare Sergius for a few moments? Raina has hardly seen him yet. Perhaps I can help you to settle about the regiments.

SERGIUS [*protesting*] My dear madam, impossible: you—

CATHERINE [*stopping him playfully*] You stay here, my dear Sergius: theres no hurry. I have a word or two to say to Paul. [*Sergius instantly bows and steps back*]. Now, dear [*taking Petkoff's arm*]: come and see the electric bell.

PETKOFF. Oh, very well, very well.

They go into the house together affectionately. Sergius, left alone with Raina, looks anxiously at her, fearing that she is still offended. She smiles, and stretches out her arms to him.

SERGIUS [*hastening to her*] Am I forgiven?

RAINA [*placing her hands on his shoulders as she looks up at him with admiration and worship*] My hero! My king!

SERGIUS. My queen! [*He kisses her on the forehead*].

RAINA. How I have envied you, Sergius! You have been out in the world, on the field of battle, able to prove yourself there worthy of any woman in the world; whilst I have had to sit at home inactive—dreaming—useless—doing nothing that could give me the right to call myself worthy of any man.

SERGIUS. Dearest: all my deeds have been yours. You inspired me. I have gone through the war like a knight in a tournament with his lady looking down at him!

RAINA. And you have never been absent from my thoughts for a moment. [*Very solemnly*] Sergius: I think we two have found the higher love. When I think of you, I feel that I could never do a base deed, or think an ignoble thought.

SERGIUS. My lady and my saint! [*He clasps her reverently*].

RAINA [*returning his embrace*] My lord and my—

SERGIUS. Sh—sh! Let me be the worshipper, dear. You little know how unworthy even the best man is of a girl's pure passion!

RAINA. I trust you. I love you. You will never disappoint me,

Sergius. [*Louka is heard singing within the house. They quickly release each other*]. I cant pretend to talk indifferently before her: my heart is too full. [*Louka comes from the house with her tray. She goes to the table, and begins to clear it, with her back turned to them*]. I will get my hat; and then we can go out until lunch time. Wouldnt you like that?

SERGIUS. Be quick. If you are away five minutes, it will seem five hours. [*Raina runs to the top of the steps, and turns there to exchange looks with him and wave him a kiss with both hands. He looks after her with emotion for a moment; then turns slowly away, his face radiant with the loftiest exaltation. The movement shifts his field of vision, into the corner of which there now comes the tail of Louka's double apron. His attention is arrested at once. He takes a stealthy look at her, and begins to twirl his moustache mischievously, with his left hand akimbo on his hip. Finally, striking the ground with his heels in something of a cavalry swagger, he strolls over to the other side of the table, opposite her, and says*] Louka: do you know what the higher love is?

LOUKA [*astonished*] No, sir.

SERGIUS. Very fatiguing thing to keep up for any length of time, Louka. One feels the need of some relief after it.

LOUKA [*innocently*] Perhaps you would like some coffee, sir? [*She stretches her hand across the table for the coffee pot*].

SERGIUS [*taking her hand*] Thank you, Louka.

LOUKA [*pretending to pull*] Oh, sir, you know I didnt mean that. I'm surprised at you!

SERGIUS [*coming clear of the table and drawing her with him*] I am surprised at myself, Louka. What would Sergius, the hero of Slivnitza, say if he saw me now? What would Sergius, the apostle of the higher love, say if he saw me now? What would the half dozen Sergiuses who keep popping in and out of this handsome figure of mine say if they caught us here? [*Letting go her hand and slipping his arm dexterously round her waist*] Do you consider my figure handsome, Louka?

LOUKA. Let me go, sir. I shall be disgraced. [*She struggles: he holds her inexorably*]. Oh, will you let go?

SERGIUS [*looking straight into her eyes*] No.

LOUKA. Then stand back where we cant be seen. Have you no common sense?

SERGIUS. Ah! thats reasonable. [*He takes her into the stableyard gateway, where they are hidden from the house*].

LOUKA [*plaintively*] I may have been seen from the windows: Miss Raina is sure to be spying about after you.

SERGIUS [*stung: letting her go*] Take care, Louka. I may be worthless enough to betray the higher love; but do not you insult it.

LOUKA [*demurely*] Not for the world, sir, I'm sure. May I go on with my work, please, now?

SERGIUS [*again putting his arm round her*] You are a provoking little witch, Louka. If you were in love with me, would you spy out of windows on me?

LOUKA. Well, you see, sir, since you say you are half a dozen different gentlemen all at once, I should have a great deal to look after.

SERGIUS [*charmed*] Witty as well as pretty. [*He tries to kiss her*].

LOUKA [*avoiding him*] No: I dont want your kisses. Gentlefolk are all alike: you making love to me behind Miss Raina's back; and she doing the same behind yours.

SERGIUS [*recoiling a step*] Louka!

LOUKA. It shews how little you really care.

SERGIUS [*dropping his familiarity, and speaking with freezing politeness*] If our conversation is to continue, Louka, you will please remember that a gentleman does not discuss the conduct of the lady he is engaged to with her maid.

LOUKA. It's so hard to know what a gentleman considers right. I thought from your trying to kiss me that you had given up being so particular.

SERGIUS [*turning from her and striking his forehead as he comes back into the garden from the gateway*] Devil! devil!

LOUKA. Ha! ha! I expect one of the six of you is very like me, sir; though I am only Miss Raina's maid. [*She goes back to her work at the table, taking no further notice of him*].

SERGIUS [*speaking to himself*] Which of the six is the real man? thats the question that torments me. One of them is a hero, another a buffoon, another a humbug, another perhaps a bit of a black-guard. [*He pauses, and looks furtively at Louka as he adds, with deep bitterness*] And one, at least, is a coward: jealous, like all cowards. [*He goes to the table*]. Louka.

LOUKA. Yes?

SERGIUS. Who is my rival?

LOUKA. You shall never get that out of me, for love or money.

SERGIUS. Why?

LOUKA. Never mind why. Besides, you would tell that I told you; and I should lose my place.

SERGIUS [*holding out his right hand in affirmation*] No! on the honor of a—[*He checks himself; and his hand drops, nerveless, as he concludes sardonically*]—of a man capable of behaving as I have been behaving for the last five minutes. Who is he?

LOUKA. I dont know. I never saw him. I only heard his voice through the door of her room.

SERGIUS. Damnation! How dare you?

LOUKA [*retreating*] Oh, I mean no harm: youve no right to take up my words like that. The mistress knows all about it. And I tell you that if that gentleman ever comes here again, Miss Raina will marry him, whether he likes it or not. I know the difference be-tween the sort of manner you and she put on before one another and the real manner.

Sergius shivers as if she had stabbed him. Then, setting his face like iron, he strides grimly to her, and grips her above the elbows with both hands.

SERGIUS. Now listen you to me.

LOUKA [*wincing*] Not so tight: youre hurting me.

SERGIUS. That doesnt matter. You have stained my honor by making me a party to your eavesdropping. And you have be-trayed your mistress.

LOUKA [*writhing*] Please—

SERGIUS. That shews that you are an abominable little clod of common clay, with the soul of a servant. [*He lets her go as if she were an unclean thing, and turns away, dusting his hands of her, to the bench by the wall, where he sits down with averted head, meditating gloomily*].

LOUKA [*whimpering angrily with her hands up her sleeves, feeling her bruised arms*] You know how to hurt with your tongue as well as with your hands. But I dont care, now Ive found out that whatever clay I'm made of, youre made of the same. As for her, she's a liar; and her fine airs are a cheat; and I'm worth six of her. [*She shakes the pain off hardily; tosses her head; and sets to work to put the things on the tray*].

He looks doubtfully at her. She finishes packing the tray, and laps the cloth over the edges, so as to carry all out together. As she stoops to lift it, he rises.

SERGIUS. Louka! [*She stops and looks defiantly at him*]. A gentleman has no right to hurt a woman under any circumstances. [*With profound humility, uncovering his head*] I beg your pardon.

LOUKA. That sort of apology may satisfy a lady. Of what use is it to a servant?

SERGIUS [*rudely crossed in his chivalry, throws it off with a bitter laugh, and says slightingly*] Oh! you wish to be paid for the hurt? [*He puts on his shako, and takes some money from his pocket*].

LOUKA [*her eyes filling with tears in spite of herself*] No: I want my hurt made well.

SERGIUS [*sobered by her tone*] How?

She rolls up her left sleeve; clasps her arm with the thumb and fingers of her right hand; and looks down at the bruise. Then she raises her head and looks straight at him. Finally, with a superb gesture, she presents her arm to be kissed. Amazed, he looks at her; at the arm; at her again; hesitates; and then, with shuddering intensity, exclaims Never! *and gets away as far as possible from her.*

Her arm drops. Without a word, and with unaffected dignity, she takes her tray, and is approaching the house when Raina returns, wearing a hat and jacket in the height of the Vienna fashion of the previous year, 1885. *Louka makes way proudly for her, and then goes into the house.*

RAINA. I'm ready. Whats the matter? [*Gaily*] Have you been flirting with Louka?

SERGIUS [*hastily*] No, no. How can you think such a thing?

RAINA [*ashamed of herself*] Forgive me, dear: it was only a jest. I am so happy today.

He goes quickly to her, and kisses her hand remorsefully. Catherine comes out and calls to them from the top of the steps.

CATHERINE [*coming down to them*] I am sorry to disturb you, children; but Paul is distracted over those three regiments. He doesnt know how to send them to Philippopolis; and he objects to every suggestion of mine. You must go and help him, Sergius. He is in the library.

RAINA [*disappointed*] But we are just going out for a walk.

SERGIUS. I shall not be long. Wait for me just five minutes. [*He runs up the steps to the door*].

RAINA [*following him to the foot of the steps and looking up at him with timid coquetry*] I shall go round and wait in full view of the library windows. Be sure you draw father's attention to me. If you are a moment longer than five minutes, I shall go in and fetch you, regiments or no regiments.

SERGIUS [*laughing*] Very well. [*He goes in*].

Raina watches him until he is out of her sight. Then, with a perceptible relaxation of manner, she begins to pace up and down the garden in a brown study.

CATHERINE. Imagine their meeting that Swiss and hearing the whole story! The very first thing your father asked for was the old coat we sent him off in. A nice mess you have got us into!

RAINA [*gazingly thoughtfully at the gravel as she walks*] The little beast!

CATHERINE. Little beast! What little beast?

RAINA. To go and tell! Oh, if I had him here, I'd cram him with chocolate creams till he couldnt ever speak again!

CATHERINE. Dont talk such stuff. Tell me the truth, Raina. How long was he in your room before you came to me?

RAINA [*whisking round and recommencing her march in the opposite direction*] Oh, I forget.

CATHERINE. You cannot forget! Did he really climb up after the soldiers were gone; or was he there when that officer searched the room?

RAINA. No. Yes: I think he must have been there then.

CATHERINE. You t h i n k! Oh, Raina! Raina! Will anything ever make you straightforward? If Sergius finds out, it will be all over between you.

RAINA [*with cool impertinence*] Oh, I know Sergius is your pet. I sometimes wish you could marry him instead of me. You would just suit him. You would pet him, and spoil him, and mother him to perfection.

CATHERINE [*opening her eyes very widely indeed*] Well, upon my word!

RAINA [*capriciously: half to herself*] I always feel a longing to do or say something dreadful to him—to shock his propriety—to scandalize the five senses out of him. [*To Catherine, perversely*] I dont care whether he finds out about the chocolate cream soldier or not. I half hope he may. [*She again turns and strolls flippantly away up the path to the corner of the house*].

CATHERINE. And what should I be able to say to your father, pray?

RAINA [*over her shoulder, from the top of the two steps*] Oh, poor father! As if he could help himself! [*She turns the corner and passes out of sight*].

CATHERINE [*looking after her, her fingers itching*] Oh, if you were only ten years younger! [*Louka comes from the house with a salver, which she carries hanging down by her side*]. Well?

LOUKA. Theres a gentleman just called, madam. A Serbian officer.

CATHERINE [*flaming*] A Serb! And how dare he—[*checking herself bitterly*] Oh, I forgot. We are at peace now. I suppose we shall have them calling every day to pay their compliments. Well: if he is an officer why dont you tell your master? He is in the library with Major Saranoff. Why do you come to me?

LOUKA. But he asks for you, madam. And I dont think he knows who you are: he said the lady of the house. He gave me this little ticket for you. [*She takes a card out of her bosom; puts it on the salver; and offers it to Catherine*].

CATHERINE [*reading*] "Captain Bluntschli"? Thats a German name.

LOUKA. Swiss, madam, I think.

CATHERINE [*with a bound that makes Louka jump back*] Swiss! What is he like?

LOUKA [*timidly*] He has a big carpet bag, madam.

CATHERINE. Oh Heavens! he's come to return the coat. Send him away: say we're not at home: ask him to leave his address and I'll write to him. Oh stop: that will never do. Wait! [*She throws herself into a chair to think it out. Louka waits*]. The master and Major Saranoff are busy in the library, arnt they?

LOUKA. Yes, madam.

CATHERINE [*decisively*] Bring the gentleman out here at once. [*Peremptorily*] And be very polite to him. Dont delay. Here [*impatiently snatching the salver from her*]: leave that here; and go straight back to him.

LOUKA. Yes, madam [*going*].

CATHERINE. Louka!

LOUKA [*stopping*] Yes, madam.

CATHERINE. Is the library door shut?

LOUKA. I think so, madam.

CATHERINE. If not, shut it as you pass through.

LOUKA. Yes, madam [*going*].

CATHERINE. Stop! [*Louka stops*]. He will have to go that way [*indicating the gate of the stableyard*]. Tell Nicola to bring his bag here after him. Dont forget.

LOUKA [*surprised*] His bag?

CATHERINE. Yes: here: as soon as possible. [*Vehemently*] Be quick! [*Louka runs into the house. Catherine snatches her apron off and throws it behind a bush. She then takes up the salver and uses it as a mirror, with the result that the handkerchief tied round her head follows the apron. A touch to her hair and a shake to her dressing gown make her presentable*]. Oh, how? how? h o w can a man be such a fool! Such a moment to select! [*Louka appears at the door of the house, announcing* Captain Bluntschli. *She stands aside at the top of the steps to let him pass before she goes in again. He is the man of the midnight adventure in Raina's room, clean, well brushed, smartly uniformed, and out of trouble, but still unmistakeably the same man. The moment Louka's back is turned, Catherine swoops on him with impetuous, urgent, coaxing appeal*]. Captain Bluntschli: I am very glad to see you; but you must leave this house at once. [*He raises his eyebrows*]. My husband has just returned with my future son-in-law; and they know nothing. If they did, the consequences would be terrible. You are a foreigner: you do not feel our national animosities as we do. We still hate the Serbs: the effect of the peace on my husband has been to make him feel like a lion baulked of his prey. If he discovers our secret, he will never forgive me; and my daughter's life will hardly be safe. Will you, like the chivalrous gentleman and soldier you are, leave at once before he finds you here?

BLUNTSCHLI [*disappointed, but philosophical*] At once, gracious lady. I only came to thank you and return the coat you lent me. If you will allow me to take it out of my bag and leave it with your servant as I pass out, I need detain you no further. [*He turns to go into the house*].

CATHERINE [*catching him by the sleeve*] Oh, you must not think of going back that way. [*Coaxing him across to the stable gates*] This is the shortest way out. Many thanks. So glad to have been of service to you. Goodbye.

BLUNTSCHLI. But my bag?

CATHERINE. It shall be sent on. You will leave me your address.

BLUNTSCHLI. True. Allow me. [*He takes out his card-case, and stops to write his address, keeping Catherine in an agony of im-*

patience. *As he hands her the card, Petkoff, hatless, rushes from the house in a fluster of hospitality, followed by Sergius*].

PETKOFF [*as he hurries down the steps*] My dear Captain Bluntschli—

CATHERINE. Oh Heavens! [*She sinks on the seat against the wall*].

PETKOFF [*too preoccupied to notice her as he shakes Bluntschli's hand heartily*] Those stupid people of mine thought I was out here, instead of in the—haw!—library [*he cannot mention the library without betraying how proud he is of it*]. I saw you through the window. I was wondering why you didnt come in. Saranoff is with me: you remember him, dont you?

SERGIUS [*saluting humorously, and then offering his hand with great charm of manner*] Welcome, our friend the enemy!

PETKOFF. No longer the enemy, happily. [*Rather anxiously*] I hope youve called as a friend, and not about horses or prisoners.

CATHERINE. Oh, quite as a friend, Paul. I was just asking Captain Bluntschli to stay to lunch; but he declares he must go at once.

SERGIUS [*sardonically*] Impossible, Bluntschli. We want you here badly. We have to send on three cavalry regiments to Philippopolis; and we dont in the least know how to do it.

BLUNTSCHLI [*suddenly attentive and businesslike*] Philippopolis? The forage is the trouble, I suppose.

PETKOFF [*eagerly*] Yes: thats it. [*To Sergius*] He sees the whole thing at once.

BLUNTSCHLI. I think I can shew you how to manage that.

SERGIUS. Invaluable man! Come along! [*Towering over Bluntschli, he puts his hand on his shoulder and takes him to the steps, Petkoff following*].

Raina comes from the house as Bluntschli puts his foot on the first step.

RAINA. Oh! The chocolate cream soldier!

Bluntschli stands rigid. Sergius, amazed, looks at Raina, then at Petkoff, who looks back at him and then at his wife.

CATHERINE [*with commanding presence of mind*] My dear Raina, dont you see that we have a guest here? Captain Bluntschli: one of our new Serbian friends.

Raina bows: Bluntschli bows.

RAINA. How silly of me! [*She comes down into the centre of the group, between Bluntschli and Petkoff*]. I made a beautiful ornament this morning for the ice pudding; and that stupid Nicola has just put down a pile of plates on it and spoilt it. [*To Bluntschli, winningly*] I hope you didnt think that you were the chocolate cream soldier, Captain Bluntschli.

BLUNTSCHLI [*laughing*] I assure you I did. [*Stealing a whimsical glance at her*] Your explanation was a relief.

PETKOFF [*suspiciously, to Raina*] And since when, pray, have y o u taken to cooking?

CATHERINE. Oh, whilst you were away. It is her latest fancy.

PETKOFF [*testily*] And has Nicola taken to drinking? He used to be careful enough. First he shews Captain Bluntschli out here when he knew quite well I was in the library; and then he goes downstairs and breaks Raina's chocolate soldier. He must— [*Nicola appears at the top of the steps with the bag. He descends; places it respectfully before Bluntschli; and waits for further orders. General amazement. Nicola, unconscious of the effect he is producing, looks perfectly satisfied with himself. When Petkoff recovers his power of speech, he breaks out at him with*] Are you mad, Nicola?

NICOLA [*taken aback*] Sir?

PETKOFF. What have you brought that for?

NICOLA. My lady's orders, major. Louka told me that—

CATHERINE [*interrupting him*] My orders! Why should I order you to bring Captain Bluntschli's luggage out here? What are you thinking of, Nicola?

NICOLA [*after a moment's bewilderment, picking up the bag as he addresses Bluntschli with the very perfection of servile discretion*] I beg your pardon, captain, I am sure. [*To Catherine*] My fault, madam: I hope youll overlook it. [*He bows, and is going to the steps with the bag, when Petkoff addresses him angrily*].

PETKOFF. Youd better go and slam that bag, too, down on Miss Raina's ice pudding! [*This is too much for Nicola. The bag drops from his hand almost on his master's toes, eliciting a roar of*] Begone, you butter-fingered donkey.

NICOLA [*snatching up the bag, and escaping into the house*] Yes, major.

CATHERINE. Oh, never mind, Paul: dont be angry.

PETKOFF [*blustering*] Scoundrel! He's got out of hand while I was away. I'll teach him. Infernal blackguard! The sack next Saturday! I'll clear out the whole establishment—[*He is stifled by the caresses of his wife and daughter, who hang round his neck, petting him*].

CATHERINE | [*together*] | Now, now, now, it mustnt be angry.
RAINA | | Wow, wow, wow: not on your first
He meant no harm. Be good to please me, dear.
day at home. I'll make another ice pudding.
Sh-sh-sh-sh!
Tch-ch-ch!

PETKOFF [*yielding*] Oh well, never mind. Come, Bluntschli: lets have no more nónsense about going away. You know very well youre not going back to Switzerland yet. Until you do go back youll stay with us.

RAINA. Oh, do, Captain Bluntschli.

PETKOFF [*to Catherine*] Now, Catherine: it's of you he's afraid. Press him; and he'll stay.

CATHERINE. Of course I shall be only too delighted if [*appealingly*] Captain Bluntschli really wishes to stay. He knows my wishes.

BLUNTSCHLI [*in his driest military manner*] I am at madam's orders.

SERGIUS [*cordially*] That settles it!

PETKOFF [*heartily*] Of course!

RAINA. You see you m u s t stay.

BLUNTSCHLI [*smiling*] Well, if I must, I must.

Gesture of despair from Catherine.

ACT III

In the library after lunch. It is not much of a library. Its literary equipment consists of a single fixed shelf stocked with old paper covered novels, broken backed, coffee stained, torn and thumbed; and a couple of little hanging shelves with a few gift books on them: the rest of the wall space being occupied by trophies of war and the chase. But it is a most comfortable sitting room. A row of three large windows shews a mountain panorama, just now seen in one of its friendliest aspects in the mellowing afternoon light. In the corner next the right hand window a square earthenware stove, a perfect tower of glistening pottery, rises nearly to the ceiling and guarantees plenty of warmth. The ottoman is like that in Raina's room, and similarly placed; and the window seats are luxurious with decorated cushions. There is one object, however, hopelessly out of keeping with its surroundings. This is a small kitchen table, much the worse for wear, fitted as a writing table with an old canister full of pens, an eggcup filled with ink, and a deplorable scrap of heavily used pink blotting paper.

At the side of this table, which stands to the left of anyone facing the window, Bluntschli is hard at work with a couple of maps before him, writing orders. At the head of it sits Sergius, who is supposed to be also at work, but is actually gnawing the feather of a pen, and contemplating Bluntschli's quick, sure, businesslike progress with a mixture of envious irritation at his own incapacity and awestruck wonder at an ability which seems to him almost miraculous, though its prosaic character forbids him to esteem it. The Major is comfortably established on the ottoman, with a newspaper in his hand and the tube of his hookah within easy reach. Catherine sits at the stove, with her back to them, embroidering. Raina, reclining on the divan, is gazing in a daydream out at the Balkan landscape, with a neglected novel in her lap.

The door is on the same side as the stove, farther from the window. The button of the electric bell is at the opposite side, behind Bluntschli.

PETKOFF [*looking up from his paper to watch how they are getting on at the table*] Are you sure I cant help you in any way, Bluntschli?

BLUNTSCHLI [*without interrupting his writing or looking up*] Quite sure, thank you. Saranoff and I will manage it.

SERGIUS [*grimly*] Yes: we'll manage it. He finds out what to do; draws up the orders; and I sign em. Division of labor! [*Bluntschli passes him a paper*]. Another one? Thank you. [*He plants the paper squarely before him; sets his chair carefully parallel to it; and signs with his cheek on his elbow and his protruded tongue following the movements of his pen*]. This hand is more accustomed to the sword than to the pen.

PETKOFF. It's very good of you, Bluntschli: it is indeed, to let yourself be put upon in this way. Now are you q u i t e sure I can do nothing?

CATHERINE [*in a low warning tone*] You can stop interrupting, Paul.

PETKOFF [*starting and looking round at her*] Eh? Oh! Quite right, my love: quite right. [*He takes his newspaper up again, but presently lets it drop*]. Ah, you havnt been campaigning, Catherine: you dont know how pleasant it is for us to sit here, after a good lunch, with nothing to do but enjoy ourselves. Theres only one thing I want to make me thoroughly comfortable.

CATHERINE. What is that?

PETKOFF. My old coat. I'm not at home in this one: I feel as if I were on parade.

CATHERINE. My dear Paul, how absurd you are about that old coat! It must be hanging in the blue closet where you left it.

PETKOFF. My dear Catherine, I tell you Ive looked there. Am I to believe my own eyes or not? [*Catherine rises and crosses the room to press the button of the electric bell*]. What are you shewing off that bell for? [*She looks at him majestically, and silently resumes her chair and her needlework*]. My dear: if you think the obstinacy of your sex can make a coat out of two old dressing gowns of Raina's, your waterproof, and my mackintosh, youre mistaken. Thats exactly what the blue closet contains at present.

Nicola presents himself.

CATHERINE. Nicola: go to the blue closet and bring your master's old coat here: the braided one he wears in the house.

NICOLA. Yes, madame. [*He goes out*].

PETKOFF. Catherine.

CATHERINE. Yes, Paul.

PETKOFF. I bet you any piece of jewellery you like to order from Sofia against a week's housekeeping money that the coat isnt there.

CATHERINE. Done, Paul!

PETKOFF [*excited by the prospect of a gamble*] Come: heres an opportunity for some sport. Wholl bet on it? Bluntschli: I'll give you six to one.

BLUNTSCHLI [*imperturbably*] It would be robbing you, major. Madame is sure to be right. [*Without looking up, he passes another batch of papers to Sergius*].

SERGIUS [*also excited*] Bravo, Switzerland! Major: I bet my best charger against an Arab mare for Raina that Nicola finds the coat in the blue closet.

PETKOFF [*eagerly*] Your best char—

CATHERINE [*hastily interrupting him*] Dont be foolish, Paul. An Arabian mare will cost you 50,000 levas.

RAINA [*suddenly coming out of her picturesque revery*] Really, mother, if you are going to take the jewellery, I dont see why you should grudge me my Arab.

Nicola comes back with the coat, and brings it to Petkoff, who can hardly believe his eyes.

CATHERINE. Where was it, Nicola?

NICOLA. Hanging in the blue closet, madame.

PETKOFF. Well, I am d—

CATHERINE [*stopping him*] Paul!

PETKOFF. I could have sworn it wasnt there. Age is beginning to tell on me. I'm getting hallucinations. [*To Nicola*] Here: help me to change. Excuse me, Bluntschli. [*He begins changing coats, Nicola acting as valet*]. Remember: I didnt take that bet of yours,

Sergius. Youd better give Raina that Arab steed yourself, since youve roused her expectations. Eh, Raina? [*He looks round at her; but she is again rapt in the landscape. With a little gush of parental affection and pride, he points her out to them, and says*] She's dreaming, as usual.

SERGIUS. Assuredly she shall not be the loser.

PETKOFF. So much the better for her. *I* shant come off so cheaply, I expect. [*The change is now complete. Nicola goes out with the discarded coat*]. Ah, now I feel at home at last. [*He sits down and takes his newspaper with a grunt of relief*].

BLUNTSCHLI [*to Sergius, handing a paper*] Thats the last order.

PETKOFF [*jumping up*] What! Finished?

BLUNTSCHLI. Finished.

PETKOFF [*with childlike envy*] Havnt you anything for m e to sign?

BLUNTSCHLI. Not necessary. His signature will do.

PETKOFF [*inflating his chest and thumping it*] Ah well, I think weve done a thundering good day's work. Can I do anything more?

BLUNTSCHLI. You had better both see the fellows that are to take these. [*Sergius rises*] Pack them off at once; and shew them that Ive marked on the orders the time they should hand them in by. Tell them that if they stop to drink or tell stories—if theyre five minutes late, theyll have the skin taken off their backs.

SERGIUS [*stiffening indignantly*] I'll say so. [*He strides to the door*]. And if one of them is man enough to spit in my face for insulting him, I'll buy his discharge and give him a pension. [*He goes out*].

BLUNTSCHLI [*confidentially*] Just see that he talks to them properly, major, will you?

PETKOFF [*officiously*] Quite right, Bluntschli, quite right. I'll see to it. [*He goes to the door importantly, but hesitates on the threshold*]. By the bye, Catherine, you may as well come too. Theyll be far more frightened of you than of me.

CATHERINE [*putting down her embroidery*] I daresay I had better.

You would only splutter at them. [*She goes out, Petkoff holding the door for her and following her*].

BLUNTSCHLI. What an army! They make cannons out of cherry trees; and the officers send for their wives to keep discipline! [*He begins to fold and docket the papers*].

Raina, who has risen from the divan, marches slowly down the room with her hands clasped behind her, and looks mischievously at him.

RAINA. You look ever so much nicer than when we last met. [*He looks up, surprised*]. What have you done to yourself?

BLUNTSCHLI. Washed; brushed; good night's sleep and breakfast. Thats all.

RAINA. Did you get back safely that morning?

BLUNTSCHLI. Quite, thanks.

RAINA. Were they angry with you for running away from Sergius's charge?

BLUNTSCHLI [*grinning*] No: they were glad; because theyd all just run away themselves.

RAINA [*going to the table, and leaning over it towards him*] It must have made a lovely story for them: all that about me and my room.

BLUNTSCHLI. Capital story. But I only told it to one of them: a particular friend.

RAINA. On whose discretion you could absolutely rely?

BLUNTSCHLI. Absolutely.

RAINA. Hm! He told it all to my father and Sergius the day you exchanged the prisoners. [*She turns away and strolls carelessly across to the other side of the room*].

BLUNTSCHLI [*deeply concerned, and half incredulous*] No! You dont mean that, do you?

RAINA [*turning, with sudden earnestness*] I do indeed. But they dont know that it was in this house you took refuge. If Sergius knew, he would challenge you and kill you in a duel.

BLUNTSCHLI. Bless me! then dont tell him.

RAINA. Please be serious, Captain Bluntschli. Can you not

realize what it is to me to deceive him? I want to be quite perfect with Sergius: no meanness, no smallness, no deceit. My relation to him is the one really beautiful and noble part of my life. I hope you can understand that.

BLUNTSCHLI [*sceptically*] You mean that you wouldnt like him to find out that the story about the ice pudding was a—a—a— You know.

RAINA [*wincing*] Ah, dont talk of it in that flippant way. I lied: I know it. But I did it to save your life. He would have killed you. That was the second time I ever uttered a falsehood. [*Bluntschli rises quickly and looks doubtfully and somewhat severely at her*]. Do you remember the first time?

BLUNTSCHLI. I! No. Was I present?

RAINA. Yes; and I told the officer who was searching for you that you were not present.

BLUNTSCHLI. True. I should have remembered it.

RAINA [*greatly encouraged*] Ah, it is natural that you should forget it first. It cost you nothing: it cost me a lie! A lie!

She sits down on the ottoman, looking straight before her with her hands clasped round her knee. Bluntschli, quite touched, goes to the ottoman with a particularly reassuring and considerate air, and sits down beside her.

BLUNTSCHLI. My dear young lady, dont let this worry you. Remember: I'm a soldier. Now what are the two things that happen to a soldier so often that he comes to think nothing of them? One is hearing people tell lies [*Raina recoils*]: the other is getting his life saved in all sorts of ways by all sorts of people.

RAINA [*rising in indignant protest*] And so he becomes a creature incapable of faith and of gratitude.

BLUNTSCHLI [*making a wry face*] Do you like gratitude? I dont. If pity is akin to love, gratitude is akin to the other thing.

RAINA. Gratitude! [*Turning on him*] If you are incapable of gratitude you are incapable of any noble sentiment. Even animals are grateful. Oh, I see now exactly what you think of me! You were not surprised to hear me lie. To you it was something I probably did every day! every hour!! That is how men think of women. [*She paces the room tragically*].

BLUNTSCHLI [*dubiously*] Theres reason in everything. You said youd told only two lies in your whole life. Dear young lady: isnt that rather a short allowance? I'm quite a straightforward man myself; but it wouldnt last me a whole morning.

RAINA [*staring haughtily at him*] Do you know, sir, that you are insulting me?

BLUNTSCHLI. I cant help it. When you strike that noble attitude and speak in that thrilling voice, I admire you; but I find it impossible to believe a single word you say.

RAINA [*superbly*] Captain Bluntschli!

BLUNTSCHLI [*unmoved*] Yes?

RAINA [*standing over him, as if she could not believe her senses*] Do you mean what you said just now? Do you know what you said just now?

BLUNTSCHLI. I do.

RAINA [*gasping*] I! I!!!! [*She points to herself incredulously, meaning "I, Raina Petkoff tell lies!" He meets her gaze unflinchingly. She suddenly sits down beside him, and adds, with a complete change of manner from the heroic to a babyish familiarity*] How did you find me out?

BLUNTSCHLI [*promptly*] Instinct, dear young lady. Instinct, and experience of the world.

RAINA [*wonderingly*] Do you know, you are the first man I ever met who did not take me seriously?

BLUNTSCHLI. You mean, dont you, that I am the first man that has ever taken you quite seriously?

RAINA. Yes: I suppose I do mean that. [*Cosily, quite at her ease with him*] How strange it is to be talked to in such a way! You know, Ive always gone on like that.

BLUNTSCHLI. You mean the—?

RAINA. I mean the noble attitude and the thrilling voice. [*They laugh together*]. I did it when I was a tiny child to my nurse. She

believed in it. I do it before my parents. They believe in it. I do it
before Sergius. He believes in it.

BLUNTSCHLI. Yes: he's a little in that line himself, isnt he?

RAINA [*startled*] Oh! Do you think so?

BLUNTSCHLI. You know him better than I do.

RAINA. I wonder—I wonder is he? If I thought that—! [*Discouraged*] Ah, well: what does it matter? I suppose, now youve
found me out, you despise me.

BLUNTSCHLI [*warmly, rising*] No, my dear young lady, no, no,
no a thousand times. It's part of your youth: part of your charm.
I'm like all the rest of them: the nurse, your parents, Sergius: I'm
your infatuated admirer.

RAINA [*pleased*] Really?

BLUNTSCHLI [*slapping his breast smartly with his hand, German
fashion*] Hand aufs Herz! Really and truly.

RAINA [*very happy*] But what did you think of me for giving
you my portrait?

BLUNTSCHLI [*astonished*] Your portrait! You never gave me
your portrait.

RAINA [*quickly*] Do you mean to say you never got it?

BLUNTSCHLI. No. [*He sits down beside her, with renewed interest,
and says, with some complacency*] When did you send it to me?

RAINA [*indignantly*] I did not send it to you. [*She turns her
head away, and adds, reluctantly*] It was in the pocket of that
coat.

BLUNTSCHLI [*pursing his lips and rounding his eyes*] Oh-o-oh!
I never found it. It must be there still.

RAINA [*springing up*] There still! for my father to find the first
time he puts his hand in his pocket! Oh, how could you be so
stupid?

BLUNTSCHLI [*rising also*] It doesnt matter: I suppose it's only a
photograph: how can he tell who it was intended for? Tell him
he put it there himself.

RAINA [*bitterly*] Yes: that is so clever! isnt it? [*Distractedly*] Oh!
what shall I do?

BLUNTSCHLI. Ah, I see. You wrote something on it. That was rash.

RAINA [*vexed almost to tears*] Oh, to have done such a thing for you, who care no more—except to laugh at me—oh! Are you sure nobody has touched it?

BLUNTSCHLI. Well. I cant be quite sure. You see, I couldnt carry it about with me all the time: one cant take much luggage on active service.

RAINA. What did you do with it?

BLUNTSCHLI. When I got through to Pirot I had to put it in safe keeping somehow. I thought of the railway cloak room; but thats the surest place to get looted in modern warfare. So I pawned it.

RAINA. Pawned it!!!

BLUNTSCHLI. I know it doesnt sound nice; but it was much the safest plan. I redeemed it the day before yesterday. Heaven only knows whether the pawnbroker cleared out the pockets or not.

RAINA [*furious: throwing the words right into his face*] You have a low shopkeeping mind. You think of things that would never come into a gentleman's head.

BLUNTSCHLI [*phlegmatically*] Thats the Swiss national character, dear lady. [*He returns to the table*].

RAINA. Oh, I wish I had never met you. [*She flounces away, and sits at the window fuming*].

Louka comes in with a heap of letters and telegrams on her salver, and crosses, with her bold free gait, to the table. Her left sleeve is looped up to the shoulder with a brooch, shewing her naked arm, with a broad gilt bracelet covering the bruise.

LOUKA [*to Bluntschli*] For you. [*She empties the salver with a fling on to the table*]. The messenger is waiting. [*She is determined not to be civil to an enemy, even if she must bring him his letters*].

BLUNTSCHLI [*to Raina*] Will you excuse me: the last postal delivery that reached me was three weeks ago. These are the subsequent accumulations. Four telegrams: a week old. [*He opens one*]. Oho! Bad news!

RAINA [*rising and advancing a little remorsefully*] Bad news?

BLUNTSCHLI. My father's dead. [*He looks at the telegram with his lips pursed, musing on the unexpected change in his arrangements. Louka crosses herself hastily*].

RAINA. Oh, how very sad!

BLUNTSCHLI. Yes: I shall have to start for home in an hour. He has left a lot of big hotels behind him to be looked after. [*He takes up a fat letter in a long blue envelope*]. Here's a whacking letter from the family solicitor. [*He pulls out the enclosures and glances over them*]. Great Heavens! Seventy! Two hundred! [*In a crescendo of dismay*] Four hundred! Four thousand!! Nine thousand six hundred!!! What on earth am I to do with them all?

RAINA [*timidly*] Nine thousand hotels?

BLUNTSCHLI. Hotels! nonsense. If you only knew! Oh, it's too ridiculous! Excuse me: I must give my fellow orders about starting. [*He leaves the room hastily, with the documents in his hand*].

LOUKA [*knowing instinctively that she can annoy Raina by disparaging Bluntschli*] He has not much heart, that Swiss. He has not a word of grief for his poor father.

RAINA [*bitterly*] Grief! A man who has been doing nothing but killing people for years! What does he care? What does any soldier care? [*She goes to the door, restraining her tears with difficulty*].

LOUKA. Major Saranoff has been fighting too; and he has plenty of heart left. [*Raina, at the door, draws herself up haughtily and goes out*]. Aha! I thought you wouldnt get much feeling out of your soldier. [*She is following Raina when Nicola enters with an armful of logs for the stove*].

NICOLA [*grinning amorously at her*] Ive been trying all the afternoon to get a minute alone with you, my girl. [*His countenance changes as he notices her arm*]. Why, what fashion is that of wearing your sleeve, child?

LOUKA [*proudly*] My own fashion.

NICOLA. Indeed! If the mistress catches you, she'll talk to you. [*He puts the logs down, and seats himself comfortably on the ottoman*].

LOUKA. Is that any reason why you should take it on yourself to talk to me?

NICOLA. Come! dont be so contrairy with me. Ive some good news for you. [*She sits down beside him. He takes out some paper money. Louka, with an eager gleam in her eyes, tries to snatch it; but he shifts it quickly to his left hand, out of her reach*]. See! a twenty leva bill! Sergius gave me that, out of pure swagger. A fool and his money are soon parted. Theres ten levas more. The Swiss gave me that for backing up the mistress's and Raina's lies about him. He's no fool, he isnt. You should have heard old Catherine downstairs as polite as you please to me, telling me not to mind the Major being a little impatient; for they knew what a good servant I was—after making a fool and a liar of me before them all! The twenty will go to our savings; and you shall have the ten to spend if youll only talk to me so as to remind me I'm a human being. I get tired of being a servant occasionally.

LOUKA. Yes: sell your manhood for 30 levas, and buy me for 10! [*Rising scornfully*] Keep your money. You were born to be a servant. I was not. When you set up your shop you will only be everybody's servant instead of somebody's servant. [*She goes moodily to the table and seats herself regally in Sergius's chair*].

NICOLA [*picking up his logs, and going to the stove*] Ah, wait til you see. We shall have our evenings to ourselves; and I shall be master in my own house, I promise you. [*He throws the logs down and kneels at the stove*].

LOUKA. You shall never be master in mine.

NICOLA [*turning, still on his knees, and squatting down rather forlornly on his calves, daunted by her implacable disdain*] You have a great ambition in you, Louka. Remember: if any luck comes to you, it was I that made a woman of you.

LOUKA. You!

NICOLA [*scrambling up and going at her*] Yes, me. Who was it made you give up wearing a couple of pounds of false black hair on your head and reddening your lips and cheeks like any other Bulgarian girl! I did. Who taught you to trim your nails, and keep your hands clean, and be dainty about yourself, like a fine Russian lady? Me: do you hear that? me! [*She tosses her head defiantly; and he turns away, adding, more coolly*] Ive often thought that if Raina were out of the way, and you just a little less of a fool and Sergius just a little more of one, you might come to be one of my grandest customers, instead of only being my wife and costing me money.

LOUKA. I believe you would rather be my servant than my husband. You would make more out of me. Oh, I know that soul of yours.

NICOLA [*going closer to her for greater emphasis*] Never you mind my soul; but just listen to my advice. If you want to be a lady, your present behavior to me wont do at all, unless when we're alone. It's too sharp and impudent; and impudence is a sort of familiarity: it shews affection for me. And dont you try being high and mighty with me, either. Youre like all country girls: you think it's genteel to treat a servant the way I treat a stableboy. Thats only your ignorance; and dont you forget it. And dont be so ready to defy everybody. Act as if you expected to have your own way, not as if you expected to be ordered about. The way to get on as a lady is the same as the way to get on as a servant: youve got to know your place: thats the secret of it. And you may depend on me to know my place if you get promoted. Think over it, my girl. I'll stand by you: one servant should always stand by another.

LOUKA [*rising impatiently*] Oh, I must behave in my own way. You take all the courage out of me with your cold-blooded wisdom. Go and put those logs on the fire: thats the sort of thing you understand.

Before Nicola can retort, Sergius comes in. He checks himself a moment on seeing Louka; then goes to the stove.

SERGIUS [*to Nicola*] I am not in the way of your work, I hope.

NICOLA [*in a smooth, elderly manner*] Oh no, sir: thank you kindly. I was only speaking to this foolish girl about her habit of running up here to the library whenever she gets a chance, to look at the books. Thats the worst of her education, sir: it gives her habits above her station. [*To Louka*] Make that table tidy, Louka, for the Major. [*He goes out sedately*].

Louka, without looking at Sergius, pretends to arrange the papers on the table. He crosses slowly to her, and studies the arrangement of her sleeve reflectively.

SERGIUS. Let me see: is there a mark there? [*He turns up the bracelet and sees the bruise made by his grasp. She stands motionless, not looking at him: fascinated, but on her guard*]. Ffff! Does it hurt?

LOUKA. Yes.

SERGIUS. Shall I cure it?

LOUKA [*instantly withdrawing herself proudly, but still not looking at him*] No. You cannot cure it now.

SERGIUS [*masterfully*] Quite sure? [*He makes a movement as if to take her in his arms*].

LOUKA. Dont trifle with me, please. An officer should not trifle with a servant.

SERGIUS [*indicating the bruise with a merciless stroke of his forefinger*] That was no trifle, Louka.

LOUKA [*flinching; then looking at him for the first time*] Are you sorry?

SERGIUS [*with measured emphasis, folding his arms*] I am never sorry.

LOUKA [*wistfully*] I wish I could believe a man could be as unlike a woman as that. I wonder are you really a brave man?

SERGIUS [*unaffectedly, relaxing his attitude*] Yes: I am a brave man. My heart jumped like a woman's at the first shot; but in the charge I found that I was brave. Yes: that at least is real about me.

LOUKA. Did you find in the charge that the men whose fathers are poor like mine were any less brave than the men who are rich like you?

SERGIUS [*with bitter levity*] Not a bit. They all slashed and cursed and yelled like heroes. Psha! the courage to rage and kill is cheap. I have an English bull terrier who has as much of that sort of courage as the whole Bulgarian nation, and the whole Russian nation at its back. But he lets my groom thrash him, all the same. Thats your soldier all over! No, Louka: your poor men can cut throats; but they are afraid of their officers; they put up with insults and blows; they stand by and see one another punished like children: aye, and help to do it when they are ordered. And the officers!!! Well [*with a short harsh laugh*] *I* am an officer. Oh, [*fervently*] give me the man who will defy to the death any power on earth or in heaven that sets itself up against his own will and conscience: he alone is the brave man.

LOUKA. How easy it is to talk! Men never seem to me to grow up: they all have schoolboy's ideas. You dont know what true courage is.

SERGIUS [*ironically*] Indeed! I am willing to be instructed. [*He sits on the ottoman, sprawling magnificently*].

LOUKA. Look at me! how much am I allowed to have my own will? I have to get your room ready for you: to sweep and dust, to fetch and carry. How could that degrade me if it did not degrade you to have it done for you? But [*with subdued passion*] if I were Empress of Russia, above everyone in the world, then!! Ah then, though according to you I could shew no courage at all, you should see, you should see.

SERGIUS. What would you do, most noble Empress?

LOUKA. I would marry the man I loved, which no other queen in Europe has the courage to do. If I loved you, though you would be as far beneath me as I am beneath you, I would dare to be the equal of my inferior. Would you dare as much if you loved me? No: if you felt the beginnings of love for me you would not let it grow. You would not dare: you would marry a rich man's daughter because you would be afraid of what other people would say of you.

SERGIUS [*bounding up*] You lie: it is not so, by all the stars! If I loved you, and I were the Czar himself, I would set you on the throne by my side. You know that I love another woman, a woman as high above you as heaven is above earth. And you are jealous of her.

LOUKA. I have no reason to be. She will never marry you now. The man I told you of has come back. She will marry the Swiss.

SERGIUS [*recoiling*] The Swiss!

LOUKA. A man worth ten of you. Then you can come to me; and I will refuse you. You are not good enough for me. [*She turns to the door*].

SERGIUS [*springing after her and catching her fiercely in his arms*] I will kill the Swiss; and afterwards I will do as I please with you.

LOUKA [*in his arms, passive and steadfast*] The Swiss will kill you, perhaps. He has beaten you in love. He may beat you in war.

SERGIUS [*tormentedly*] Do you think I believe that she—she! whose worst thoughts are higher than your best ones, is capable of trifling with another man behind my back?

LOUKA. Do you think she would believe the Swiss if he told her now that I am in your arms?

SERGIUS [*releasing her in despair*] Damnation! Oh, damnation! Mockery! mockery everywhere! everything I think is mocked by everything I do. [*He strikes himself frantically on the breast*]. Coward! liar! fool! Shall I kill myself like a man, or live and pretend to laugh at myself? [*She again turns to go*]. Louka! [*She stops near the door*]. Remember: you belong to me.

LOUKA [*turning*] What does that mean? An insult?

SERGIUS [*commandingly*] It means that you love me, and that I have had you here in my arms, and will perhaps have you there again. Whether that is an insult I neither know nor care: take it as you please. But [*vehemently*] I will not be a coward and a trifler. If I choose to love you, I dare marry you, in spite of all Bulgaria. If these hands ever touch you again, they shall touch my affianced bride.

LOUKA. We shall see whether you dare keep your word. And take care. I will not wait long.

SERGIUS [*again folding his arms and standing motionless in the middle of the room*] Yes: we shall see. And you shall wait my pleasure.

Bluntschli, much preoccupied, with his papers still in his hand, enters, leaving the door open for Louka to go out. He goes across to the table, glancing at her as he passes. Sergius, without altering his resolute attitude, watches him steadily. Louka goes out, leaving the door open.

BLUNTSCHLI [*absently, sitting at the table as before, and putting down his papers*] Thats a remarkable looking young woman.

SERGIUS [*gravely, without moving*] Captain Bluntschli.

BLUNTSCHLI. Eh?

SERGIUS. You have deceived me. You are my rival. I brook no rivals. At six o'clock I shall be in the drilling-ground on the Klissoura road, alone, on horseback, with my sabre. Do you understand?

BLUNTSCHLI [*staring, but sitting quite at his ease*] Oh, thank you: thats a cavalry man's proposal. I'm in the artillery; and I have the choice of weapons. If I go, I shall take a machine gun. And there shall be no mistake about the cartridges this time.

SERGIUS [*flushing, but with deadly coldness*] Take care, sir. It is not our custom in Bulgaria to allow invitations of that kind to be trifled with.

BLUNTSCHLI [*warmly*] Pooh! dont talk to me about Bulgaria. You dont know what fighting is. But have it your own way. Bring your sabre along. I'll meet you.

SERGIUS [*fiercely delighted to find his opponent a man of spirit*] Well said, Switzer. Shall I lend you my best horse?

BLUNTSCHLI. No: damn your horse! thank you all the same, my dear fellow. [*Raina comes in, and hears the next sentence*]. I shall fight you on foot. Horseback's too dangerous: I dont want to kill you if I can help it.

RAINA [*hurrying forward anxiously*] I have heard what Captain Bluntschli said, Sergius. You are going to fight. Why? [*Sergius turns away in silence, and goes to the stove, where he stands watching her as she continues, to Bluntschli*] What about?

BLUNTSCHLI. I dont know: he hasnt told me. Better not interfere, dear young lady. No harm will be done: Ive often acted as sword instructor. He wont be able to touch me; and I'll not hurt him. It will save explanations. In the morning I shall be off home; and youll never see me or hear of me again. You and he will then make it up and live happily ever after.

RAINA [*turning away deeply hurt, almost with a sob in her voice*] I never said I wanted to see you again.

SERGIUS [*striding forward*] Ha! That is a confession.

RAINA [*haughtily*] What do you mean?

SERGIUS. You love that man!

RAINA [*scandalized*] Sergius!

SERGIUS. You allow him to make love to you behind my back, just as you treat me as your affianced husband behind his. Bluntschli: you knew our relations; and you deceived me. It is for that that I call you to account, not for having received favors *I* never enjoyed.

BLUNTSCHLI [*jumping up indignantly*] Stuff! Rubbish! I have received no favors. Why, the young lady doesnt even know whether I'm married or not.

RAINA [*forgetting herself*] Oh! [*Collapsing on the ottoman*] Are you?

SERGIUS. You see the young lady's concern, Captain Bluntschli. Denial is useless. You have enjoyed the privilege of being received in her own room, late at night—

BLUNTSCHLI [*interrupting him pepperily*] Yes, you blockhead! she received me with a pistol at her head. Your cavalry were at my heels. I'd have blown out her brains if she'd uttered a cry.

SERGIUS [*taken aback*] Bluntschli! Raina: is this true?

RAINA [*rising in wrathful majesty*] Oh, how dare you, how dare you?

BLUNTSCHLI. Apologize, man: apologize. [*He resumes his seat at the table*].

SERGIUS [*with the old measured emphasis, folding his arms*] I never apologize!

RAINA [*passionately*] This is the doing of that friend of yours, Captain Bluntschli. It is he who is spreading this horrible story about me. [*She walks about excitedly*].

F

BLUNTSCHLI. No: he's dead. Burnt alive.

RAINA [*stopping, shocked*] Burnt alive!

BLUNTSCHLI. Shot in the hip in a woodyard. Couldnt drag himself out. Your fellows' shells set the timber on fire and burnt him, with half a dozen other poor devils in the same predicament.

RAINA. How horrible!

SERGIUS. And how ridiculous! Oh, war! war! the dream of patriots and heroes! A fraud, Bluntschli. A hollow sham, like love.

RAINA [*outraged*] Like love! You say that before me!

BLUNTSCHLI. Come, Saranoff: that matter is explained.

SERGIUS. A hollow sham, I say. Would you have come back here if nothing had passed between you except at the muzzle of your pistol? Raina is mistaken about your friend who was burnt. He was not my informant.

RAINA. Who then? [*Suddenly guessing the truth*] Ah, Louka! my maid! my servant! You were with her this morning all that time after—after—Oh, what sort of god is this I have been worshipping! [*He meets her gaze with sardonic enjoyment of her disenchantment. Angered all the more, she goes closer to him, and says, in a lower, intenser tone*] Do you know that I looked out of the window as I went upstairs, to have another sight of my hero; and I saw something I did not understand then. I know now that you were making love to her.

SERGIUS [*with grim humor*] You saw that?

RAINA. Only too well. [*She turns away, and throws herself on the divan under the centre window, quite overcome*].

SERGIUS [*cynically*] Raina: our romance is shattered. Life's a farce.

BLUNTSCHLI [*to Raina, whimsically*] You see: he's found himself out now.

SERGIUS [*going to him*] Bluntschli: I have allowed you to call me a blockhead. You may now call me a coward as well. I refuse to fight you. Do you know why?

BLUNTSCHLI. No; but it doesnt matter. I didnt ask the reason when you cried on; and I dont ask the reason now that you cry off. I'm a professional soldier: I fight when I have to, and am very glad to get out of it when I havnt to. Youre only an amateur: you think fighting's an amusement.

SERGIUS [*sitting down at the table, nose to nose with him*] You shall hear the reason all the same, my professional. The reason is that it takes two men—real men—men of heart, blood and honor —to make a genuine combat. I could no more fight with you than I could make love to an ugly woman. Youve no magnetism: youre not a man: youre a machine.

BLUNTSCHLI [*apologetically*] Quite true, quite true. I always was that sort of chap. I'm very sorry.

SERGIUS. Psha!

BLUNTSCHLI. But now that youve found that life isnt a farce, but something quite sensible and serious, what further obstacle is there to your happiness?

RAINA [*rising*] You are very solicitous about my happiness and his. Do you forget his new love—Louka? It is not you that he must fight now, but his rival, Nicola.

SERGIUS. Rival!! [*bounding half across the room*].

RAINA. Dont you know that theyre engaged?

SERGIUS. Nicola! Are fresh abysses opening? Nicola!!

RAINA [*sarcastically*] A shocking sacrifice, isnt it? Such beauty! such intellect! such modesty! wasted on a middle-aged servant man. Really, Sergius, you cannot stand by and allow such a thing. It would be unworthy of your chivalry.

SERGIUS [*losing all self control*] Viper! Viper! [*He rushes to and fro, raging*].

BLUNTSCHLI. Look here, Saranoff: youre getting the worst of this.

RAINA [*getting angrier*] Do you realize what he has done, Captain Bluntschli? He has set this girl as a spy on us; and her reward is that he makes love to her.

SERGIUS. False! Monstrous!

RAINA. Monstrous! [*Confronting him*] Do you deny that she told you about Captain Bluntschli being in my room?

SERGIUS. No; but—

RAINA [*interrupting*] Do you deny that you were making love to her when she told you?

SERGIUS. No; but I tell you—

RAINA [*cutting him short contemptuously*] It is unnecessary to tell us anything more. That is quite enough for us. [*She turns away from him and sweeps majestically back to the window*].

BLUNTSCHLI [*quietly, as Sergius, in an agony of mortification, sinks on the ottoman, clutching his averted head between his fists*] I told you you were getting the worst of it, Saranoff.

SERGIUS. Tiger cat!

RAINA [*running excitedly to Bluntschli*] You hear this man calling me names, Captain Bluntschli?

BLUNTSCHLI. What else can he do, dear lady? He must defend himself somehow. Come [*very persuasively*]: dont quarrel. What good does it do?

Raina, with a gasp, sits down on the ottoman, and after a vain effort to look vexedly at Bluntschli, falls a victim to her sense of humor, and actually leans back babyishly against the writhing shoulder of Sergius.

SERGIUS. Engaged to Nicola! Ha! ha! Ah well, Bluntschli, you are right to take this huge imposture of a world coolly.

RAINA [*quaintly to Bluntschli, with an intuitive guess at his state of mind*] I daresay you think us a couple of grown-up babies, dont you?

SERGIUS [*grinning savagely*] He does: he does. Swiss civilization nursetending Bulgarian barbarism, eh?

BLUNTSCHLI [*blushing*] Not at all, I assure you. I'm only very glad to get you two quieted. There! there! let's be pleasant and talk it over in a friendly way. Where is this other young lady?

RAINA. Listening at the door, probably.

SERGIUS [*shivering as if a bullet had struck him, and speaking with quiet but deep indignation*] I will prove that that, at least, is a calumny. [*He goes with dignity to the door and opens it. A yell of fury bursts from him as he looks out. He darts into the passage, and returns dragging in Louka, whom he flings violently against the table, exclaiming*] Judge her, Bluntschli. You, the cool impartial man: judge the eavesdropper.

Louka stands her ground, proud and silent.

BLUNTSCHLI [*shaking his head*] I musnt judge her. I once listened myself outside a tent when there was a mutiny brewing. It's all a question of the degree of provocation. My life was at stake.

LOUKA. My love was at stake. I am not ashamed.

RAINA [*contemptuously*] Your love! Your curiosity, you mean.

LOUKA [*facing her and retorting her contempt with interest*] My love, stronger than anything you can feel, even for your chocolate cream soldier.

SERGIUS [*with quick suspicion, to Louka*] What does that mean?

LOUKA [*fiercely*] It means—

SERGIUS [*interrupting her slightingly*] Oh, I remember: the ice pudding. A paltry taunt, girl!

Major Petkoff enters, in his shirtsleeves.

PETKOFF. Excuse my shirtsleeves, gentlemen. Raina: somebody has been wearing that coat of mine: I'll swear it. Somebody with a differently shaped back. It's all burst open at the sleeve. Your mother is mending it. I wish she'd make haste: I shall catch cold. [*He looks more attentively at them*]. Is anything the matter?

RAINA. No. [*She sits down at the stove, with a tranquil air*].

SERGIUS. Oh no. [*He sits down at the end of the table, as at first*].

BLUNTSCHLI [*who is already seated*] Nothing. Nothing.

PETKOFF [*sitting down on the ottoman in his old place*] Thats all right. [*He notices Louka*]. Anything the matter, Louka?

LOUKA. No, sir.

PETKOFF [*genially*] Thats all right. [*He sneezes*]. Go and ask your mistress for my coat, like a good girl, will you?

Nicola enters with the coat. Louka makes a pretence of having business in the room by taking the little table with the hookah away to the wall near the windows.

RAINA [*rising quickly as she sees the coat on Nicola's arm*] Here it is, papa. Give it to me, Nicola; and do you put some more wood on the fire. [*She takes the coat, and brings it to the Major, who stands up to put it on. Nicola attends to the fire*].

PETKOFF [*to Raina, teasing her affectionately*] Aha! Going to be very good to poor old papa just for one day after his return from the wars, eh?

RAINA [*with solemn reproach*] Ah, how can you say that to me, father?

PETKOFF. Well, well, only a joke, little one. Come: give me a kiss. [*She kisses him*]. Now give me the coat.

RAINA. No: I am going to put it on for you. Turn your back. [*He turns his back and feels behind him with his arms for the sleeves. She dexterously takes the photograph from the pocket and throws it on the table before Bluntschli, who covers it with a sheet of paper under the very nose of Sergius, who looks on amazed, with his suspicions roused in the highest degree. She then helps Petkoff on with his coat*]. There, dear! Now are you comfortable?

PETKOFF. Quite, little love. Thanks. [*He sits down; and Raina returns to her seat near the stove*]. Oh, by the bye, Ive found something funny. Whats the meaning of this? [*He puts his hand into the picked pocket*]. Eh? Hallo! [*He tries the other pocket*]. Well, I could have sworn—! [*Much puzzled, he tries the breast pocket*]. I wonder—[*trying the original pocket*]. Where can it—? [*He rises, exclaiming*] Your mother's taken it!

RAINA [*very red*] Taken what?

PETKOFF. Your photograph, with the inscription: "Raina, to her Chocolate Cream Soldier: a Souvenir." Now you know theres something more in this than meets the eye; and I'm going to find it out. [*Shouting*] Nicola!

NICOLA [*coming to him*] Sir!

PETKOFF. Did you spoil any pastry of Miss Raina's this morning?

NICOLA. You heard Miss Raina say that I did, sir.

PETKOFF. I know that, you idiot. Was it true?

NICOLA. I am sure Miss Raina is incapable of saying anything that is not true, sir.

PETKOFF. Are you? Then I'm not. [*Turning to the others*] Come: do you think I dont see it all? [*He goes to Sergius, and slaps him on the shoulder*]. Sergius: youre the chocolate cream soldier, arnt you?

SERGIUS [*starting up*] I! A chocolate cream soldier! Certainly not.

PETKOFF. Not! [*He looks at them. They are all very serious and very conscious*]. Do you mean to tell me that Raina sends things like that to other men?

SERGIUS [*enigmatically*] The world is not such an innocent place as we used to think, Petkoff.

BLUNTSCHLI [*rising*] It's all right, Major. I'm the chocolate cream soldier. [*Petkoff and Sergius are equally astonished*]. The gracious young lady saved my life by giving me chocolate creams when I was starving: shall I ever forget their flavor! My late friend Stolz told you the story at Pirot. I was the fugitive.

PETKOFF. You! [*He gasps*]. Sergius: do you remember how those two women went on this morning when we mentioned it? [*Sergius smiles cynically. Petkoff confronts Raina severely*]. Youre a nice young woman, arnt you?

RAINA [*bitterly*] Major Saranoff has changed his mind. And when I wrote that on the photograph, I did not know that Captain Bluntschli was married.

BLUNTSCHLI [*startled into vehement protest*] I'm not married.

RAINA [*with deep reproach*] You said you were.

BLUNTSCHLI. I did not. I positively did not. I never was married in my life.

PETKOFF [*exasperated*] Raina: will you kindly inform me, if I am not asking too much, which of these gentlemen you are engaged to?

RAINA. To neither of them. This young lady [*introducing Louka, who faces them all proudly*] is the object of Major Saranoff's affections at present.

PETKOFF. Louka! Are you mad, Sergius? Why, this girl's engaged to Nicola.

NICOLA. I beg your pardon, sir. There is a mistake. Louka is not engaged to me.

PETKOFF. Not engaged to you, you scoundrel! Why, you had twenty-five levas from me on the day of your betrothal; and she had that gilt bracelet from Miss Raina.

NICOLA [*with cool unction*] We gave it out so, sir. But it was only to give Louka protection. She had a soul above her station; and I have been no more than her confidential servant. I intend, as you know, sir, to set up a shop later on in Sofia; and I look forward to her custom and recommendation should she marry into the nobility. [*He goes out with impressive discretion, leaving them all staring after him*].

PETKOFF [*breaking the silence*] Well, I am—hm!

SERGIUS. This is either the finest heroism or the most crawling baseness. Which is it, Bluntschli?

BLUNTSCHLI. Never mind whether it's heroism or baseness. Nicola's the ablest man Ive met in Bulgaria. I'll make him manager of a hotel if he can speak French and German.

LOUKA [*suddenly breaking out at Sergius*] I have been insulted by everyone here. You set them the example. You owe me an apology.

Sergius, like a repeating clock of which the spring has been touched, immediately begins to fold his arms.

BLUNTSCHLI [*before he can speak*] It's no use. He never apologizes.

LOUKA. Not to you, his equal and his enemy. To me, his poor servant, he will not refuse to apologize.

SERGIUS [*approvingly*] You are right. [*He bends his knee in his grandest manner*] Forgive me.

LOUKA. I forgive you. [*She timidly gives him her hand, which he kisses*]. That touch makes me your affianced wife.

SERGIUS [*springing up*] Ah! I forgot that.

LOUKA [*coldly*] You can withdraw if you like.

SERGIUS. Withdraw! Never! You belong to me. [*He puts his arm about her*].

Catherine comes in and finds Louka in Sergius's arms, with all the rest gazing at them in bewildered astonishment.

CATHERINE. What does this mean?

Sergius releases Louka.

PETKOFF. Well, my dear, it appears that Sergius is going to marry Louka instead of Raina. [*She is about to break out indignantly at him: he stops her by exclaiming testily*] Dont blame m e: I v e nothing to do with it. [*He retreats to the stove*].

CATHERINE. Marry Louka! Sergius: you are bound by your word to us!

SERGIUS [*folding his arms*] Nothing binds me.

BLUNTSCHLI [*much pleased by this piece of common sense*] Saranoff: your hand. My congratulations. These heroics of yours have their practical side after all. [*To Louka*] Gracious young lady: the best wishes of a good Republican! [*He kisses her hand, to Raina's great disgust, and returns to his seat*].

CATHERINE. Louka: you have been telling stories.

LOUKA. I have done Raina no harm.

CATHERINE [*haughtily*] Raina!

Raina, equally indignant, almost snorts at the liberty.

LOUKA. I have a right to call her Raina: she calls me Louka. I told Major Saranoff she would never marry him if the Swiss gentleman came back.

BLUNTSCHLI [*rising, much surprised*] Hallo!

LOUKA [*turning to Raina*] I thought you were fonder of him than of Sergius. You know best whether I was right.

BLUNTSCHLI. What nonsense! I assure you, my dear Major, my dear Madame, the gracious young lady simply saved my life, nothing else. She never cared two straws for me. Why, bless my heart and soul, look at the young lady and look at me. She, rich, young, beautiful, with her imagination full of fairy princes and noble natures and cavalry charges and goodness knows what! And I, a commonplace Swiss soldier who hardly knows what

a decent life is after fifteen years of barracks and battles: a vaga-
bond, a man who has spoiled all his chances in life through an
incurably romantic disposition, a man—

SERGIUS [*starting as if a needle had pricked him and interrupting
Bluntschli in incredulous amazement*] Excuse me, Bluntschli: what
did you say had spoiled your chances in life?

BLUNTSCHLI [*promptly*] An incurably romantic disposition. I
ran away from home twice when I was a boy. I went into the
army instead of into my father's business. I climbed the balcony
of this house when a man of sense would have dived into the
nearest cellar. I came sneaking back here to have another look at
the young lady when any other man of my age would have sent
the coat back—

PETKOFF. My coat!

BLUNTSCHLI. —yes: thats the coat I mean—would have sent
it back and gone quietly home. Do you suppose I am the sort
of fellow a young girl falls in love with? Why, look at our ages!
I'm thirty-four: I dont suppose the young lady is much over
seventeen. [*This estimate produces a marked sensation, all the rest
turning and staring at one another. He proceeds innocently*] All that
adventure which was life or death to me, was only a schoolgirl's
game to her—chocolate creams and hide and seek. Heres the
proof! [*He takes the photograph from the table*]. Now, I ask you,
would a woman who took the affair seriously have sent me this
and written on it "Raina, to her Chocolate Cream Soldier: a
Souvenir"? [*He exhibits the photograph triumphantly, as if it settled
the matter beyond all possibility of refutation*].

PETKOFF. Thats what I was looking for. How the deuce did
it get there? [*He comes from the stove to look at it, and sits down
on the ottoman*].

BLUNTSCHLI [*to Raina, complacently*] I have put everything
right, I hope, gracious young lady.

RAINA [*going to the table to face him*] I quite agree with your
account of yourself. You are a romantic idiot. [*Bluntschli is
unspeakably taken aback*]. Next time, I hope you will know the

difference between a schoolgirl of seventeen and a woman of twenty-three.

BLUNTSCHLI [*stupefied*] Twenty-three!

Raina snaps the photograph contemptuously from his hand; tears it up; throws the pieces in his face; and sweeps back to her former place.

SERGIUS [*with grim enjoyment of his rival's discomfiture*] Bluntschli: my one last belief is gone. Your sagacity is a fraud, like everything else. You have less sense than even I!

BLUNTSCHLI [*overwhelmed*] Twenty-three! Twenty-three!! [*He considers*]. Hm! [*Swiftly making up his mind and coming to his host*] In that case, Major Petkoff, I beg to propose formally to become a suitor for your daughter's hand, in place of Major Saranoff retired.

RAINA. You dare!

BLUNTSCHLI. If you were twenty-three when you said those things to me this afternoon, I shall take them seriously.

CATHERINE [*loftily polite*] I doubt, sir, whether you quite realize either my daughter's position or that of Major Sergius Saranoff, whose place you propose to take. The Petkoffs and the Saranoffs are known as the richest and most important families in the country. Our position is almost historical: we can go back for twenty years.

PETKOFF. Oh, never mind that, Catherine. [*To Bluntschli*] We should be most happy, Bluntschli, if it were only a question of your position; but hang it, you know, Raina is accustomed to a very comfortable establishment. Sergius keeps twenty horses.

BLUNTSCHLI. But who wants twenty horses? We're not going to keep a circus.

CATHERINE [*severely*] My daughter, sir, is accustomed to a first-rate stable.

RAINA. Hush, mother: youre making me ridiculous.

BLUNTSCHLI. Oh well, if it comes to a question of an establishment, here goes! [*He darts impetuously to the table; seizes the papers in the blue envelope; and turns to Sergius*]. How many horses did you say?

SERGIUS. Twenty, noble Switzer.

BLUNTSCHLI. I have two hundred horses. [*They are amazed*]. How many carriages?

SERGIUS. Three.

BLUNTSCHLI. I have seventy. Twenty-four of them will hold twelve inside, besides two on the box, without counting the driver and conductor. How many tablecloths have you?

SERGIUS. How the deuce do I know?

BLUNTSCHLI. Have you four thousand?

SERGIUS. No.

BLUNTSCHLI. I have. I have nine thousand six hundred pairs of sheets and blankets, with two thousand four hundred eider-down quilts. I have ten thousand knives and forks, and the same quantity of dessert spoons. I have three hundred servants. I have six palatial establishments, besides two livery stables, a tea gardens, and a private house. I have four medals for distinguished services; I have the rank of an officer and the standing of a gentleman; and I have three native languages. Shew me any man in Bulgaria that can offer as much!

PETKOFF [*with childish awe*] Are you Emperor of Switzerland?

BLUNTSCHLI. My rank is the highest known in Switzerland: I am a free citizen.

CATHERINE. Then, Captain Bluntschli, since you are my daughter's choice—

RAINA [*mutinously*] He's not.

CATHERINE [*ignoring her*]—I shall not stand in the way of her happiness. [*Petkoff is about to speak*] That is Major Petkoff's feeling also.

PETKOFF. Oh, I shall be only too glad. Two hundred horses! Whew!

SERGIUS. What says the lady?

RAINA [*pretending to sulk*] The lady says that he can keep his tablecloths and his omnibuses. I am not here to be sold to the highest bidder. [*She turns her back on him*].

BLUNTSCHLI. I wont take that answer. I appealed to you as a

fugitive, a beggar, and a starving man. You accepted me. You gave me your hand to kiss, your bed to sleep in, and your roof to shelter me.

RAINA. I did not give them to the Emperor of Switzerland.

BLUNTSCHLI. Thats just what I say. [*He catches her by the shoulders and turns her face-to-face with him*]. Now tell us whom you did give them to.

RAINA [*succumbing with a shy smile*] To my chocolate cream soldier.

BLUNTSCHLI [*with a boyish laugh of delight*] Thatll do. Thank you. [*He looks at his watch and suddenly becomes businesslike*]. Time's up, Major. Youve managed those regiments so well that youre sure to be asked to get rid of some of the infantry of the Timok division. Send them home by way of Lom Palanka. Saranoff: dont get married until I come back: I shall be here punctually at five in the evening on Tuesday fortnight. Gracious ladies [*his heels click*] good evening. [*He makes them a military bow, and goes*].

SERGIUS. What a man! Is he a man!

GENERAL INTRODUCTION TO THE WORKS OF
BERNARD SHAW

By A. C. Ward

GEORGE BERNARD SHAW, the greatest of the many Irishmen who have written fine plays in the English language, was born in Dublin on 26 July 1856. His father, George Carr Shaw, the youngest son in a family of thirteen children, became a minor official in the Dublin law courts, but after a few years he retired on a small pension and went into business unsuccessfully as a corn merchant. He married the daughter of an Irish landowner, who soon found that her husband was a drunkard and incapable of earning enough money to provide for her and the three children who were born to them, George Bernard Shaw and his two sisters.

Mrs Shaw had a remarkably good singing voice, and from her and her friends young Bernard learned much good operatic music, and this was to be very useful to him afterwards. When he was sixteen his mother and sisters left Dublin and went to live permanently in London, where Mrs Shaw supported herself and her daughters by giving music lessons and singing at concerts.

In the meantime Bernard Shaw had been to school in Dublin until he was fifteen. He then became a clerk and cashier in a land agent's office there until April 1876, when he followed his mother to London. When he understood that his father was unqualified to be the controlling head of the family, and that his mother was more devoted to music than to her children, he developed that extraordinary independence of mind and spirit which was to enable him, as a man, to look upon mankind and its affairs without being swayed either by custom or by other people's conventional ideas of right and wrong.

Though he received little mother-love from Mrs Shaw, the love of music that he gained from her soon proved itself useful in London, where one of his first regular positions when he took up journalism was as music critic on the *Star*, a London evening newspaper. Both as a critic of music and, a few years later, as a critic of plays for the *Saturday Review*, a weekly periodical, he wrote essays of very high quality which are still read and praised, more than fifty years after they were first printed.

When Shaw himself turned to the writing of plays, he heard with the inner ear of a musician the words that he set down to be spoken by the actors, and his sentences consequently run with a rhythmical ease that makes them easy and pleasant to speak and hear. It is for this reason that the many very long speeches in Shaw's plays are able to hold our attention, whereas speeches of a similar length by other modern playwrights are often tedious, even though the subjects they deal with may be as important as Shaw's. The finest example of the influence of opera on his dramatic work is Act III of *Man and Superman*, of which more will be said below.

After settling in London, Bernard Shaw found it very difficult to live by writing, and for the first ten years he had to rely mainly upon his mother for food and lodging. Yet during those years he was laying the foundations of his career, joining political societies and addressing public meetings, sometimes at street corners. One day in September 1884 he went to a hall in the City of London to hear a lecture by the American economist Henry George (author of a well-known book, *Progress and Poverty*) who advocated that national revenue should be raised by a single tax on land values, instead of by numerous taxes on a variety of things. Henry George's lecture converted Shaw to Socialism, and almost at once he joined the newly-founded Fabian Society. The Fabians wanted to bring about a gradual evolutionary change, not a sudden and violent revolutionary one, from capitalism to socialism, and they had a powerful influence on British political life during the next forty or fifty years.

Round about the time Shaw joined the Fabian Society he also met Mrs Annie Besant, whose ardent support of independence for India did much to make the British public aware that the

Indian people's desire for political freedom could not be ignored. Mrs Besant was a great admirer of Shaw, and she soon joined him as a member of the Fabian Society, until her enthusiasm and energies were diverted to the support of Theosophy. She made herself the English leader of the theosophists and strengthened her ties with India through the theosophists there.

In his early years as a socialist Bernard Shaw believed that if the condition of civilized societies was to be improved, it must be done by legislation aiming at equality, reducing in various ways the fortunes of the rich in order to help and uplift the poor. Though he continued to preach equality for the remainder of his long life, as he grew older he trusted less in the power of Acts of Parliament to increase human welfare and happiness. He came round to the opinion that the first thing required in the making of a Good Society is not so much good laws as good men and women—men and women, that is, who are righteous in spirit and not merely well-intentioned and kind-hearted. Good people will make good laws, but good laws passed by a few do not necessarily make a good society.

While he was still a boy, Shaw had abandoned the Christian religion as it was practised by the churches, which he believed had strayed far from the teachings of Christ. But though he would not call himself a Christian, many of his strongest convictions and most of his personal conduct were those of a religious man. His sense of the sacredness of life, animal as well as human; his purity of living—he ate no flesh, drank no alcohol, smoked no tobacco; his kindness and generosity to his fellows (though he opposed charity on the ground that it was usually only a cheap substitute for social justice); his insistence that it is the duty of all men to strive to leave the world a better place than they found it, to hand on to future generations the torch of life burning more brightly—all these beliefs, though Shaw would have claimed that they were based on reason not on faith, were so powerful in him as a guide to conduct that they had the force of a religion.

He became a vegetarian when he was twenty-five. His reading

G

of the works of the English poet Shelley had some influence in leading him to refrain from eating meat, but the stronger motive was his deep feeling that 'animals are our fellow creatures', not to be slain for human food.

Politics and journalism occupied Bernard Shaw until 1898, when he reached the age of forty-two. His first attempts at creative literary work produced five unsuccessful novels between 1879 and 1883, and in 1885 he made his first attempt to write a play, but left it unfinished. Seven years later he completed it and on 9 December 1892 it was performed in London. Called *Widowers' Houses*, this play dealt with the evils of London slums, in which at that time many filthy and decaying houses were owned by landlords who lived at ease elsewhere on the rents squeezed from poor and wretched tenants.

A play on such a subject—on, that is, a genuine social evil—was something entirely new in the English theatres. It had no success, and when in the following years Shaw went on to write other plays about real human problems, such as prostitution (*Mrs Warren's Profession*), war (*Arms and the Man*), religious intolerance (*The Devil's Disciple*), revenge (*Captain Brassbound's Conversion*), and so on, he was extremely unpopular with many people, and years were to pass before his plays brought him enough money to live on. For a gradually increasing number of people, however, he became a leader in new ways of thought and a champion of intellectual freedom.

Until Bernard Shaw began to write for the theatre, there had been no modern British dramatist who took current social, political, and religious problems as subjects for plays. He started out with the conviction that the emotional tangles of men and women had received far too much attention on the stage, and he made up his mind to do in English what Henrik Ibsen had been doing in Norwegian since about 1875; namely, to write plays discussing public affairs which touched the lives of very large numbers of people.

Not until a season of intellectual drama was started at the Court Theatre in London in 1904 were Bernard Shaw's plays brought to the notice of a large audience. The experiment was so successful that it continued until 1907, by which time there had been 711 performances of eleven of Shaw's plays there. *John Bull's Other Island* (a comedy about Irish politics) was the first play by Shaw that became popular.

It was at the same theatre that *Man and Superman* was produced on 23 May 1905. In the character of Henry Straker, the chauffeur, it introduced a new type of working man who understood and delighted in modern machinery and was destined to be more important in the technological age then approaching than the landed aristocracy who had for centuries been the ruling class. *Man and Superman*, called by Shaw 'A Comedy and a Philosophy', is full of ideas which were then new and startling, but we can only glance here at Act III, which is a kind of dream happening to some of the characters who appear in the first two acts. Act III introduces three persons from the old Spanish legend of Don Juan — Juan himself; Donna Anna, one of the many women he loved and betrayed; and the ghost of Anna's father, whom Don Juan had killed in a duel. They meet and converse with the Devil in Hell. Mozart, the great eighteenth-century Austrian composer, wrote an opera (*Don Giovanni*) based on the Don Juan legend, and the sounds of Mozart's music were in Bernard Shaw's ears while he was writing the many extremely long speeches for this scene in Hell, which begins where Mozart's opera ends. The opinions expressed by the four characters during their argument, which lasts for about ninety minutes in performance on the stage, were invented wholly by Shaw. It is often said that the characters in his plays are merely mouthpieces for Shaw's personal opinions, but this cannot be true, because in each of his plays the different characters put forward opinions which conflict with each other, and Shaw leaves the reader (or the spectator in the theatre) to decide which is right. In the 'Don Juan in Hell' scene the Devil tries to convince the others that human beings are so stupid and bad that nothing can save them from destruction. Don Juan claims that, on the contrary, there is in Man a spirit which inspires him to struggle upward towards the evolution of the Superman, who will be far wiser and better than Man is now. That spirit is named 'the Life Force' in Bernard Shaw's plays.

The discussion between the Devil and Don Juan and the others is a serious philosophical argument such as no other dramatist would have dared to write for the stage, since no one but Shaw would have thought it possible to make an audience listen to pure argument for so long. He succeeded, partly because he could be witty and amusing and make people laugh even while he was dealing with the most serious topics, and partly because he built up his great scenes just as a composer builds up the music in an opera or a symphony. Shaw introduces a subject for discussion, then another subject a little later on—as a composer brings in one musical theme or melody after another—and soon the various subjects are woven together into a discussion which interests us intellectually and pleases us artistically.

Shaw was always deeply interested in the *sound* of words as well as in their sense and meaning. As a young man he learned shorthand and always wrote his plays in it for his secretary to type out in longhand. This choice of shorthand as a working language was due both to its time-saving advantages and to its being based on phonetics, which always uses the same symbol for the same spoken sound. Ordinary written English is extremely illogical in spelling, a confusing variety of different sounds being represented by the same letters, *e.g.* cough = kof, but plough = plow, and dough = doh, etc. This makes English harder to learn and use than it might be if a separate letter or symbol were used for every sound. Shaw spent a good deal of time trying to persuade English people to adopt an enlarged alphabet. He also wrote one of his most popular plays, *Pygmalion*, on the subject of correct pronunciation, and he directed that after he died a considerable part of the large fortune he left should be used to finance any genuine scheme for bringing into common use his enlarged alphabet and reformed spelling. But the British have so far shown no inclination to adopt Bernard Shaw's system.

From 1905, when *Man and Superman*, his first great play, was performed, Shaw was the world's most famous living playwright, though he long remained unpopular with those who disliked his advanced views and his wish to reform society. Nevertheless it was at length widely recognized that he stood second only to Shakespeare among all the British playwrights, and his writings were known and valued in all countries long before he received the Nobel Prize for Literature in 1925.

Glimpses of the religious side of Shaw's nature appear in the majority of his plays, and very clearly in *Saint Joan*, where he took Joan of Arc both as a heroine of history and as a heroine of faith. She helped to free the land of France from the English armies in the fifteenth century, and she would obey only the voice of God which, she declared, spoke to her privately. She therefore refused to submit to the authority of priests and princes when they wanted her to behave contrary to what she believed God had told her, and she was burned as a heretic, as Shaw himself probably would have been if he had lived in Joan of Arc's century, for he had the same stubborn belief in the right of individual judgment based on the voice of conscience.

Though he did not enjoy foreign travel and went abroad very little—until his friends, especially his wife, persuaded him to visit Soviet Russia in 1931 and to go in 1932–3 on a voyage round the world, during which he visited Bombay—Shaw was in the widest sense an internationalist. In exile from his own land and living in England, for whose people he had curiously mixed feelings of affection, respect, and derision, he was without racial prejudices and looked on all nations with a cool and impartial eye. He did not care particularly for any one nation as a political unit, but he was benevolent to all humanity as a matter of principle. In his eyes most political leaders were blunderers, insufficiently educated in the art of ruling, which he regarded as the highest art of all.

In spite of his intense interest in political affairs, however, Shaw will almost certainly be remembered in the future much more by his plays than by his ideas on government and public affairs. He wrote fifty plays, long and short, but his other writings (which include *The Intelligent Woman's Guide to Socialism and Capitalism* and *Everybody's Political What's What?*) are of much greater total length. The Prefaces which he added to most of the plays when they came to be printed are among the best prose essays that can be found anywhere in English literature, but their connection with the plays to which they are attached is often slight.

Shaw died in 1950, in his ninety-fifth year, having produced his last important play, *The Apple Cart*, some twenty years before, in 1929. The height of his fame was reached with *Saint Joan* in 1923, and it is most probable that this and several other of his plays will always be more highly thought of than *Back to Methuselah* (1922), which he himself regarded as his masterpiece.

Back to Methuselah, an enormously long work in five parts, fails as a play for more reasons than can be discussed within the limits of this Introduction. Its importance among Shaw's works comes from the clear statement of his 'gospel' in the Preface, and its working-out (much less clearly) in the dialogue of the five parts of the play. His gospel of Creative Evolution and his belief in the Life Force were opposed to Charles Darwin's theory of evolution by Natural Selection. In Darwin's theory the Survival of the Fittest comes about through the killing-off of the weak by the strong, but the idea of Shaw's Creative Evolution is that the fittest are those who survive by superior intelligence and by the exercise of will power. Shaw held that if we desire with passionate strength of will to be better and finer people and to live longer, in fact to be changed into Supermen, and if that strength of will is passed on to our descendants, what we desire will ultimately be brought about. The nations would then be ruled in wisdom and virtue, and war and other evils would vanish from the earth.

INTRODUCTION TO *ARMS AND THE MAN*

By A. C. Ward

THE TITLE of the first two volumes of Bernard Shaw's dramatic works, *Plays Pleasant and Unpleasant*, published in 1898, was chosen for the special purpose of showing that his plays were of a different kind from those that audiences and readers had been used to up to that time. Previously the two main divisions of drama were *tragedy* and *comedy*. In tragedy, someone had to die violently before the play ended; while in comedy there was usually plenty of amusement but not much else. But in modern life, as Shaw wanted to write about it for the stage, violent death did not play a large part, for world wars were then unthought of. He was more troubled about the many unpleasant social conditions that made life miserable for large numbers of people, and there were other disturbing though less serious aspects of society that he thought might be changed by making pleasant fun of them. He did use the words tragedy and comedy for two or three of his later plays, but even then the tragedies were not wholly tragic nor the comedies free from seriousness.

Arms and the Man, the earliest of Shaw's 'pleasant' plays, is both amusing and thought-provoking: it makes us laugh and it makes us think, for it has a serious message or messages. If we could say only 'It made people laugh and had a thought-provoking message in 1894', we should know that *Arms and the Man* was no more important than the many other plays written about the same time and now nearly all forgotten. What makes Shaw's plays better than those of his contemporaries is that both the serious and the humorous parts seem as fresh and up-to-date to-day as when he wrote them. What he saw either to frown at or to smile at were not simply the temporary injustices or passing follies of his own generation, but certain human characteristics which last from generation to generation, however much they may appear to change as time goes on.

95

The first important thing to be recognized in *Arms and the Man*, therefore, is that although it is supposed to take place in Bulgaria in 1885, with characters who are Bulgarian soldiers and their womenfolk, and a Swiss hotel-keeper's son, these facts are hardly more important than the scenery and costumes. Shaw could have chosen any other country and nationality without altering the nature and habits of the characters. An English novelist, Anthony Hope, had written, a few years before, a popular romantic tale (*The Prisoner of Zenda*) about an imaginary country he called Ruritania. This started a fashion for novels and plays with picturesque scenery and dashing uniforms and showy dresses, and anything of that kind has since been called 'Ruritanian'. Although Shaw took the name of an actual country, *Arms and the Man* is best thought of as a 'Ruritanian' play, so far as its outward appearances are concerned. Until he became famous, Shaw no more hesitated to use familiar material than Shakespeare did. Both of them aimed at kinds of originality which did not depend upon plot or scenery or costumes. A Bulgarian setting for *Arms and the Man* made a stage picture that was attractive to ordinary theatre-goers who only wanted to be amused; but having once captured their attention, Shaw then set out to make them think, and, as a reward for thinking, he also made them laugh.

What was it he wanted them—and us—to think about in connection with *Arms and the Man*? The play has two themes: one is *war*, the other is *marriage*. These themes are interwoven, for Shaw believed that while war is evil and stupid, and marriage desirable and good, both had become wrapped in romantic illusions which led to disastrous wars and also to unhappy marriages.

The romantic view of war (he held) is based on the idealistic notion that men fight because they are heroes, and that the soldier who takes the biggest risks wins the greatest glory and is the greatest hero. In *Arms and the Man* Raina Petkoff intends, at the time the play opens, to become the wife of Major Sergius Saranoff, who is then away fighting the Serbs. News has come home to Raina and her mother that Sergius has ridden bravely at the head of a victorious cavalry charge, and Raina rejoices because she can now believe that her betrothed is 'just as splendid and noble as he looks! that the world is really a glorious world for women who can see its glory and men who can act its romance!' In the opening scene of the play, after adoring Sergius's portrait, Raina goes to bed murmuring 'My hero! My hero!' This is a romantic girl's romantic view of life, but then reality suddenly breaks in upon her.

An enemy officer, in headlong retreat with the defeated Serbs, rushes into her room from the outside balcony to take refuge. He is desperate through exhaustion and fear, and Raina sneers at him. Nevertheless, when the pursuers come to search the house, Raina hides the fugitive and denies having seen him. She learns, after the pursuit is over, that he is a Swiss, fighting for the Serbs as a professional soldier; and she is again contemptuous when he tells her that instead of ammunition he carries chocolate in his cartridge cases, having found that food is more useful in battle than bullets.

At Raina's request that he should describe the great Bulgarian cavalry charge, the man tells her that its leader (whom she knows was Sergius) rode 'like an operatic tenor . . . with flashing eyes and lovely moustache . . . thinking he'd done the cleverest thing ever known, whereas he ought to be courtmartialled for it. Of all the fools ever let loose on a field of battle, that man must be the very maddest. He and his regiment simply committed suicide . . .'—or they would have committed suicide, the man goes on to say, only the Serbs had no ammunition left and therefore could not repel the charge. The scene ends with the man falling asleep through uncontrollable weariness, and Raina finds herself moved to pity by the suffering he has endured. She had imagined war as an exciting sport; she has now seen it as a dreadful reality through contact with one of the defeated.

Until the war of 1914–18 came to support the view that professional skill and caution in battle are no less desirable than physical courage, Shaw was supposed to have belittled soldiers in *Arms and the Man*; and it took two world wars to prove beyond doubt that chocolate (symbolizing all kinds of food) is as necessary to an army as cartridges.

In the later scenes of the play the other aspect of the plot comes uppermost. The war has ended and the soldiers are home again. Sergius, too, has learned something of the realities of war, and is so disgusted by them that he has sent in his resignation, saying 'Soldiering . . . is the coward's art of attacking mercilessly when you are strong, and keeping out of harm's way when you are weak.' Yet Raina continues to treat him as a hero of romance until a Captain Bluntschli comes to visit the Petkoffs' house and is discovered to be the man who took refuge in Raina's room during the retreat. In an amusing scene of the kind that is especially typical of Bernard Shaw, Bluntschli shows Raina her real character beneath the romantic mask that she has worn since childhood. Not only had she substituted an imaginary Sergius for the real one, but she had also built up an imaginary self. Bluntschli is not deceived. He says to her: 'When you strike that noble attitude and speak in that thrilling voice, I admire you; but I find it impossible to believe a word you say.' After pretending to be indignant, Raina surrenders and asks, 'How did you find me out? . . . How strange it is to be talked to in such a way! You know, Ive always gone on like that. . . . I mean the noble attitude and the thrilling voice. . . . I did it when I was a tiny child to my nurse. She believed in it. I do it before my parents. They believe in it. I do it before Sergius. He believes in it.' But her Swiss visitor does not believe in it.

Bluntschli is not deceived, either, by Sergius; nor is Sergius blind to his own true nature. When he finds himself flirting with the servant maid, Louka, immediately after an adoring love scene with Raina, he analyses himself frankly: 'I am surprised at myself, Louka. What would Sergius, the hero of Slivnitza, say if he saw me now? What would Sergius, the apostle of the higher love, say if he saw me now? What would the half-dozen Sergiuses who keep popping in and out of this handsome figure of mine say if they caught us here?'

When Raina succumbs at last to the man she calls her 'chocolate cream soldier', Bluntschli has cured her of the second of the two deceptions which ruled her life when the play began. She no longer thinks of war as a romantic game, nor does she any longer think of marriage as the mating of a beautiful heroine and a handsome hero in a lifelong romantic dream. Instead of the ornamental and fickle Sergius, she takes as her husband the plain Bluntschli, whose common sense and six hotels in Switzerland will give her stability and comfort.

The realities of love and marriage became one of the most frequent themes in Shaw's plays throughout the remainder of his long life. He thought of marriage not as a means of satisfying the personal desires of individual men and women, nor as a means of strengthening family ties, but as the means of bringing to birth a new and better generation. Though no one can predict with certainty the consequences of any marriage, Shaw never swerved from the conviction that marriage is a solemn contract, not a frivolous domestic excursion. In *Arms and the Man* and often elsewhere he laughed at this and other solemnities, but behind the humours of the relationships of Raina, Sergius, and Bluntschli lay the memories of Shaw's own childhood in a home shadowed by the failure of his own parents' marriage.

The rest of the play is mostly light-hearted fun, though amid the fun there are several shrewd hits at two sorts of snobbery: the snobbery of the manservant Nicola, who regards his employers with cynical servility, despising them, yet humbling himself before them because 'That's what they like; and that's how you'll make most out of them'; and the snobbery of the Petkoffs, who think themselves better than their neighbours because they have a library and an electric bell. As an upholder of social equality Shaw was opposed to any idea that servants are an inferior class. He held that all necessary work, however menial, is valuable as a service to the community. He also believed that it was mean and foolish to act as though the possession of wealth, or any other material advantage, is a sign of personal superiority. People may not any longer think it impressive to have an electric bell in the house, but there are countries nowadays where families with television sets and motor cars feel as stupidly proud as the Petkoffs did with their bell and library.

GENERAL NOTES

BERNARD SHAW gave careful personal attention to the printing of his plays, and for almost the whole of his career the printers, papermakers, binders, and publishers acted as his agents and carried out his instructions. The fact that he made no change in his printers after 1898 or his publishers after 1903, up to the time of his death in 1950, is a clear sign of his fair dealing and loyalty to those who served him well. He made a number of important improvements in the printing-style of plays, which had before been badly printed on cheap paper and with little care for the convenience of readers. Shaw changed all that, and most other authors, printers, and publishers of plays followed his example.

He was the first to introduce detailed descriptions of scenery, furniture, stage properties, and (most important of all) of the characters in the play. Very often these descriptions give information which is intended to help the reader to get a mental picture of the character, rather than to limit the freedom of the performer or of the stage producer. Examples of such descriptions can be found in various places in *Arms and the Man*; one that can be quoted here is the statement on page 16 that Catherine Petkoff 'is determined to be a Viennese lady', a piece of information that helps the reader to know that she is a snob trying to pretend that she is a fashionable person.

Since such descriptions and the shorter stage-directions are printed in *italic* type, Shaw avoided as far as possible the use of italics for any other purpose. Ordinarily, italics are used for printing words that are to be emphasized, but Shaw used, instead, spaced letters. Thus, if the word 'glorious' was to be emphasized in speaking the phrase 'the world is really a glorious world' he would have it printed g l o r i o u s, not *glorious*. This method not only avoided possible confusion with stage-directions in italic type, but it also represents what actually happens when we emphasize a word in speaking: we slow down our rate of speaking and the emphasized word occupies a longer time-period, just as the spaced word occupies more space on the paper when printed. But when the personal pronoun 'I' was to be emphasized, Shaw had to use the italic *I*.

Another peculiarity of Shaw's style of printing is the omission of apostrophes from contractions, such as Ive (usually printed as I've = I have), theyll (they'll = they will), shant (shan't = shall not), em ('em = them), wholl (who'll = who will), etc. This is sometimes a little confusing to the reader at first, but Shaw was thinking most of the way in which these contractions are spoken.

It will also be seen that he did not use either quotation marks or italic type for the titles of books or plays: *e.g.* Preface, page 1, has Rosmersholm, The Black Cat, A Comedy of Sighs, etc.; and in the play, Act I, page 31, has Ernani. In ordinary printing all these titles would be either in italic type or between quotation marks. (In the Introductions and Notes by the editor in this present volume, italic type is used.)

Shaw rarely printed a list of the characters at the front of the play, though this is customary in most other playwrights' printed works. (In *Arms and the Man* there does happen to be a short list of characters, in order to give the names of the first performers; but this is exceptional in Shaw.) He preferred that the reader should not be introduced to the characters by name until they appeared in the text of the play, and sometimes he did not, even in the text, print the name of a character until another character had spoken it on the stage. In *Arms and the Man* the intruding soldier is named The Man until he appears again half-way through Act II, when Catherine Petkoff reads the name aloud from the visiting-card brought in by the servant. From that point onward his name is used at the beginnings of his speeches in the printed text—Bluntschli.

For the assistance of students in other countries who have not constant access to dictionaries and other necessary reference books, the Notes in the following pages include definitions and explanations of various words and phrases which will be already familiar to English-born readers.

NOTE ON THE PREFACE TO
PLAYS PLEASANT

1. *the New Drama:* In the closing years of the nineteenth century and
   the early years of the twentieth, opinions about many things
   were changing rapidly in Britain, and the word 'new' was often
   applied to denote a change of attitude and ideas. The 'New
   Woman' meant the women who wanted to vote at parliamentary
   elections (which British women did not do at that time) and to
   earn their own living in business, or as doctors or lawyers or
   university teachers, instead of staying at home in idleness or as
   family servants. The 'New Man' is the description given by
   Shaw to the independent-minded motor mechanic and driver,
   Henry Straker, in *Man and Superman*. The 'New Morality'
   stood for the freer views on sexual relationships which were
   adopted by those who believed that Victorian puritanism and
   prudery had been harmfully repressive. The 'New Drama' was
   the general title given to the plays which dealt with the changing
   opinions about the 'new' woman, the 'new' man, the 'new'
   morality, and all the other 'new' social and political ideas. The
   'New Drama' was therefore the *intellectual drama*, of which
   Shaw was the pioneer in Britain, as Ibsen had been in Norway,
   where the 'New Drama' began.

Florence Farr: an actress who was one of the leading performers
   in the New Drama movement. Among the parts she played was
   Louka in *Arms and the Man*.

Ibsen's Rosmersholm: Ibsen lived from 1828 to 1906. Though he
   was a great poet (as in his *Brand* and *Peer Gynt*), he became
   more famous as the author of plays about social, domestic, and
   personal problems. *Rosmersholm* is one of these.

Miss A. E. F. Horniman: a wealthy English woman (1860–1937)
   who supported various theatrical schemes which helped the
   New Drama. She was responsible for putting on *Arms and the
   Man* at the Avenue Theatre, London, and she also built the famous
   Abbey Theatre in Dublin for the Irish Theatre Movement.
   Another of her valuable services was the maintenance from 1907
   to 1921 of the Gaiety Theatre, Manchester, where many new

plays were performed. A number of the dramatists and actors who first began there, afterwards became famous in London and elsewhere.

1. *the Independent Theatre:* founded in London by J. T. Grein (1862–1935) in 1891, to promote the New Drama. It was not in the usual sense a theatre, for it had no building of its own, but hired other theatres for the performances it organized. Plays by Ibsen and Shaw, among others, were produced, and (though it did not itself continue for more than a few years) the Independent Theatre led others to take up similar work.

W. B. Yeats: Irish poet and playwright who lived from 1865 to 1939. He was one of the founders of the Irish Theatre Movement and the Irish Players in Dublin, and became one of the leading poets of his time, forsaking the romantic poetry of his early period for a more symbolical and intellectual style. *Dr Todhunter* did not become well known outside Ireland.

Dryden's Virgil: The translation by John Dryden (1631–1700) of the Latin poet Virgil's epic *The Aeneid* begins, 'Arms and the man I sing', *i.e.* 'I praise the soldier and the weapons of war'. Shaw's use of the phrase as the title for his anti-heroic play gains force from the ironic twist it gives to one of the most famous lines in heroic poetry.

matinées: an Anglicized French word used to describe afternoon performances, though it originally meant something taking place in the morning.

West End theatrical management: The principal London theatres are close together in a small area of the west-end district. The supporters of the New Drama were inclined to think of the managers, or financial controllers, of those theatres as soulless men interested only in making big profits.

2. *the Renascence*, more usually spelt *Renaissance:* the revival or 'new birth' of Learning which started in Italy in the fourteenth century with Dante and others and had spread throughout western Europe by the sixteenth century.

British pre-Raphaelite painters: a mid-nineteenth-century group of artists who sought to break away from artificial styles of painting and return to the faithful representation of Nature, which they believed was the practice before Raphael, the great

Italian painter who lived from 1483 to 1520. The Pre-Raphael-
ites developed artificial mannerisms of their own and did not
last as an independent group. Their leader, John Everett Millais,
became President of the Royal Academy.

2. *William Morris and Burne-Jones:* William Morris (1834–96),
English poet, artist, craftsman, and socialist. He started a business to design and manufacture fabrics, wallpapers, furniture,
and other articles for use in houses, and they also undertook
such work as the making of stained-glass windows for churches.
Morris had an important influence on the improvement of design in Britain, and also on printing, through the Kelmscott
Press which he began in 1890 for the production of finely
printed books. The Kelmscott Chaucer is one of the finest
volumes printed in modern times. Morris was a man of great
physical energy and boundless activity and he took a prominent
part in socialist agitation. Sir Edward Burne-Jones (1833–98),
painter and designer, collaborated with Morris in stained-glass
work and other products. At one time he was thought of highly
as a painter, but his pictures have now lost much of their
attraction.

Giotto: Italian painter who lived from 1266 to 1336. He was the
pioneer of a new kind of painting which was soon to be gener-
ally adopted in Florence, where a large number of great artists
turned away from the non-realistic formal style and painted
with scientific care for natural representation. Pronounced
Jot-to.

Guild of St Matthew: a society founded in 1877 to support
Christian Socialism (see note on next page). Its founder was
Stewart Headlam (c. 1847–1924), a Church of England clergyman whom Bernard Shaw is supposed to have had in mind when
he created the character named James Mavor Morrell in *Candida.*

High Church clergymen: The Church of England tolerates various
groups with different views among its membership, the chief of
these being the Low Church group (sometimes called Evangeli-
cals) and the High Church group. The former inherits the
antagonism to the Roman Catholic Church which led to the
English Reformation in the sixteenth century, while the latter
favours pre-Reformation ritual but not the restoration in Eng-

H

land of the authority of the Pope. *Clergyman* is the English Protestant word for *priest*.

2. *an eminent Nonconformist divine:* Dr John Clifford (1836–1923) was a leader of the English religious body called Baptists, from their belief in the ceremony of adult baptism by complete immersion as necessary for admission to the company of Christians. The Baptists are one of the several 'nonconformist' groups who separated from the established Church of England in the seventeenth century, on account of their dissent from its authority and from some of its ceremonies. A *divine* is a man learned in divinity, an older word for theology.

an infidel: one who does not believe in a particular religion. In the opinion of a Christian all non-Christians are infidels, while to (for example) a Mohammedan a Christian is an infidel or unbeliever.

Sullivan: Sir Arthur Sullivan (1842–1900), English composer. He wrote some music for hymns and other religious pieces, but is much better known for his collaboration with the playwright Sir William Gilbert (1836–1911) in the melodious and comic Gilbert and Sullivan operas. The words of 'Onward, Christian Soldiers' were written by S. Baring-Gould, author of other well-known Christian hymns.

Haydn: Franz Joseph Haydn (1732–1809), world-renowned Austrian composer. *God Preserve the Emperor* ('Gott erhalte Franz den Kaiser'), the Austrian national anthem from 1797 to 1918, when new (republican) words were set to Haydn's music. Pronounced *Hyd-en.*

every drama must present a conflict: For many years it was often said that Shaw's plays ignored this basic principle of drama, but it could only be said by those who failed to see that there is in all his plays a conflict between opposing beliefs and ideas.

Christian Socialism: a nineteenth-century movement started about 1850 with the aim of uniting the socialist desire for political reform and social justice with the Christian faith of the traditionally conservative Church of England. One of its leaders was Charles Kingsley (1819–75), a prominent clergyman and famous novelist.

Widowers' Houses: Bernard Shaw's first play (1892), which deals with the evils of slum dwellings as they existed at that time.

3. *Sir George Crofts:* a character in *Mrs Warren's Profession* (written 1893–4), the third of Shaw's *Unpleasant Plays*, which was banned from the English stage until 1926.

quintessential: free from all dilution, or impurities, or non-essentials; the pure essence, heart, core, or root of a matter.

done and done with: an idiomatic phrase indicating that something is not only finished, but is put out of mind and forgotten.

the speculum of a work of art: A speculum is a mirror or some other reflecting or brilliant surface. Shaw applies the word here to that aspect of a work of art which most clearly shows its vital purpose.

'writes like an angel and talks like poor Poll': this was first said by the great English actor David Garrick (1717–79) in reference to the poet, playwright, and novelist Oliver Goldsmith (1730–1774), whose talk is said to have been foolish, though his best writings are works of genius. Garrick's actual words were:

'Here lies Nolly Goldsmith, for shortness call'd Noll,
Who wrote like an angel, but talk'd like poor Poll.'

Noll and Nolly are short for Oliver; Poll (or Polly) is the common pet name for a talking parrot.

John Ruskin: English essayist and art critic who lived from 1819 to 1900.

Carpaccio: Vittore Carpaccio (*c.* 1450–*c.* 1525), Italian painter, of the Venetian School. Pronounced *Kar-patch-ee-o.*

Bellini: Giovanni Bellini (*c.* 1428–1516), Italian painter, of the Venetian School. Pronounced *Bel-leen-ee.*

Tintoretto: Italian painter (1518–94), of the Venetian School.

Rembrandt: the greatest of the Dutch painters; lived from 1606 to 1669. Pronounced *Rem-brahnt.*

Mozart: Wolfgang Amadeus Mozart (1756–91), Austrian composer. His musical career began when he was only six years old, and although he was only thirty-five when he died, he wrote many hundreds of works, including several operas. In beauty and purity of style Mozart's music is among the greatest ever written. Pronounced *Moat-zart.*

Beethoven: Ludwig von Beethoven (1770–1827), German composer. The profundity and majesty of his symphonies and many other compositions have led to his being called 'the Shakespeare of music'. Pronounced *Bait-o-ven*.

3. *Wagner:* Richard Wagner (1813–83), German composer who brought about a revolution in the writing of operas, by making the words and drama equal in importance to the music. Bernard Shaw admired him extremely and wrote a study of his works, *The Perfect Wagnerite* (1898). Pronounced *Vahg-ner*.

Blake: William Blake (1757–1827), English poet, painter, and mystic. His works have been more highly valued in the present century than before, and Shaw is among the many modern writers and thinkers who have been influenced by Blake's revolutionary ideas on many topics.

Shelley: Percy Bysshe Shelley (1792–1822), one of the greatest of the English poets, with an unequalled lyrical gift. His unorthodox opinions on religion, morals, and politics have given him a strong hold on many later writers, including Shaw, who was attracted to vegetarianism through Shelley.

4. *incoherent:* confused; incapable of making a clear statement.

Candida: the second of Shaw's *Pleasant Plays*; written in 1894.

Aberdeen: a city on the east coast of Scotland, the inhabitants of which are jokingly said to be uncommonly fond of whisky, and to be unwilling to spend their money.

Richard Mansfield: an American actor who lived from 1857 to 1907. He was the first to perform in Shaw's plays in the United States, and he made Shaw popular there before the British had ceased to neglect him.

A Doll's House: a famous play by Ibsen, written in 1878–9. As a powerful plea for the release of women from domestic and emotional confinement it had a remarkable influence in many countries.

5. *The Man of Destiny:* the third of Shaw's *Pleasant Plays*; written in 1895. It is a short and minor piece on an episode in the life of Napoleon.

bravura: Italian word used here in the sense of *showy and without much substance*. Pronounced *brah-voora*.

You Never Can Tell: the fourth of Shaw's *Pleasant Plays*; written in 1895.

Cyril Maude. English actor-manager who lived from 1861 to 1951.

5. *Haymarket Theatre:* one of the principal London theatres and the second oldest, first built in 1720.

actor-managers: actors who also control the business side of a theatre or theatres. They have often been rebuked by authors and critics who allege that actor-managers seek only self-glorification and not the good of the drama.

Bond Street: a thoroughfare in the west-end of London where many dealers in works of art have their showrooms and galleries.

6. *backers:* a person who provides the money for the staging of a play is called the *backer*, but only if he has no regular connection with theatres and only hopes for monetary profit or some other personal benefit.

syndicates: A syndicate in this sense is a group of people who provide money jointly for the staging of plays and share any profits.

pornographic farces: plays in which the humour depends upon obscene jokes concerned with sexual relationships.

7. *Kaiser:* the title assumed by emperors of Germany until Kaiser Wilhelm II was dethroned and a republic declared in 1918. Pronounced *ky-zer*.

histrionically: in an artificial and stagy manner.

8. *pauperization:* reduction to the state of a beggar who receives money or goods without working for them.

doles: payments from charity or public funds.

Poor Law Commissioners: a body of officials appointed in Britain to administer the laws relating to persons without means of self-support, such as the unemployed, the disabled, and the aged. The Poor Laws have since been abolished and replaced by various social services which do not carry any stigma of poverty.

National Gallery: the art gallery in Trafalgar Square, London, which contains the English national collection of paintings and includes masterpieces from various countries and centuries.

British Museum: the national collection of historical and artistic objects, at Bloomsbury, London. It also includes the great libraries which attract students from every part of the world.

repertory theatres: Unlike the theatres in the west-end of London, where plays continue to run for as long as they make a profit, sometimes for two or three years, repertory theatres usually put on a different play each week. This system allows the audiences to get a better knowledge of various kinds of drama, while the players get a fuller experience, and authors have more opportunities of getting their plays performed. Repertory theatres now exist in hundreds of towns and in many districts of the large cities in Britain and other countries.

8. *would carry a knighthood with it:* a somewhat ironical allusion to the fact that in 1895 a title was given to an actor for the first time in the history of the British stage. Sir Henry Irving has since been followed by many other actor knights, and the Stage has become as respectable as the Law and the Church.

9. *Italian opera:* 'The committee plan', referred to by Shaw, was in existence at Covent Garden Theatre, London, the centre of international opera in Britain.

nuances: delicate shades of meaning, etc. Though the word is of French origin it has become Anglicized in pronunciation.

sophistication: loss of natural simplicity.

honor: for such words as honour, labour, clamour, colour, etc., Shaw used the simpler spelling which is general in America and is justified by the fact that the *u* is not sounded.

10. *over-sanguine:* too hopeful.

half guineas: 'guinea' is still used as a monetary term by the English, though there is no longer a coin so named. Its value was twenty-one shillings. A half-guinea therefore means ten shillings and six pence, which was the usual price of the best seats in London west-end theatres before 1914.

Joachim: Joseph Joachim (1831–1907), Hungarian violinist; thought by some to have been the greatest violin player that the world has ever known. He also wrote some music. Pronounced *Yoa-keem*.

beanfeasters: A beanfeast is an annual merrymaking trip to the country, or some other celebration, usually arranged for the workers in a particular factory or shop.

11. *the seamy side of life:* the darker or sordid aspect.

to brain them: to beat out their brains by violent blows, but here used by Shaw in the sense of bringing convincing evidence to disprove the arguments of a stubborn and prejudiced opponent.

12. *Moy Thomas:* novelist, dramatic critic, journalist, etc., who lived

from 1828 to 1910. He did not leave any work of lasting importance.

12. *apings:* unintelligent imitations.

Gladstone: William Ewart Gladstone (1809–98), British statesman, leader of the Liberal Party, and one of the greatest Prime Ministers.

idealism: This word, as used frequently by Shaw, is intended to suggest the falsely romantic view of life which prevents people from facing their own problems and the world's with reason and common sense.

NOTES ON *ARMS AND THE MAN*

Act I

15. *a Turkish ottoman:* an oblong padded couch serving as a divan.
16. *avalanche:* a displaced mass of ice and snow sliding down a mountain-side and carrying away whatever is in its path. Shaw uses the word here to give a vivid impression of the effect of a cavalry charge.
17. *chaff:* the husks detached from ears of corn during threshing and easily blown away.

    Byron: George Gordon, Lord Byron (1788–1824), English poet. His hatred of hypocrisy and oppression made him antagonistic to the conduct of contemporary persons and governments, though his own loose moral standards earned strong censure. He wrote stirring romantic poetry and love lyrics, as well as much biting satire. In *Don Juan*, his greatest work, he combined beautiful poetry, romantic adventures, and satire. He left England finally in 1816 and died in Greece, where he had intended to fight in the cause of independence.

    Pushkin: Alexander Sergivich Pushkin (1799–1837), the greatest of the Russian poets. He was much influenced by Byron and Shakespeare.

    cut a poor figure: compare unfavourably with others.
19. *fusillade:* rapid shooting from a number of rifles or other firearms simultaneously.
20. *unkempt:* extremely untidy, with unbrushed hair and a general appearance of neglect.

    with all his wits about him: mentally alert.
21. *cynically:* A cynic is one who adopts an attitude of sneering contempt towards mankind in general. Shaw here refers to a milder quality in Bluntschli (The Man), who is free from romantic illusions even in the presence of an attractive young woman.
22. *clamor:* loud confused noise. The normal English spelling is *clamour*.

    I'm done for: Bluntschli means that he no longer hopes to escape.
23. *feline:* cat-like; smooth-speaking, but with a sinister undertone.
24. *a narrow shave:* an escape by the narrowest margin.

24. *a miss is as good as a mile:* English proverb meaning that if the object aimed at, or the result desired, is not reached there is no consolation in knowing that it was nearly reached. Here Bluntschli is expressing relief that the Bulgarian officer just missed discovering him.

    a professional soldier: one who serves in an army not from patriotism only, but as a career and for the pay.

    you've beaten us hollow: an English idiom meaning utter defeat.

    genteel society manner: artificial and excessive politeness.

25. *superciliously:* with a contemptuous air of superiority.

26. *grub:* English slang word for food.

    shies: moves suddenly in nervous alarm.

    never smelt powder before: an English idiom still used, although it goes back to the days when the smell of gunpowder hung about a battlefield; the present-day equivalent is 'never been under fire before'.

27. *ecstatically:* used here to indicate Raina's romantically excited state.

    cannoning together: coming into violent collision.

    an operatic tenor: the hero of an opera usually sings the tenor part and is often handsome in appearance.

    Don Quixote at the windmills: In the sixteenth-century Spanish romance by Cervantes, Don Quixote is so overcome by romantic illusions that he imagines he is fighting an enemy when he is only attacking the sails of a windmill.

    as white as a sheet: pale with fear.

29. *in cold blood:* without excitement or anger or passion.

30. *a hypnotized rabbit:* rabbits are said to be struck motionless with fear when they are in the presence of danger.

    patronizingly: used here in the sense of *encouragingly.*

31. *stoop to pretend:* Raina uses this phrase to show that she thinks Bluntschli is being deliberately insincere.

    Ernani: the title of an opera by the Italian composer Giuseppi Verdi (1813–1901), first performed in Venice in 1844. Pronounced *Er-nah-nee; Vair-dee.*

32. *an old Castilian noble:* a nobleman from Castile, a province in Spain.

Act II

35. *the paling:* the fence around the garden.

     cigaret: Shaw's simplified spelling of *cigarette.*

     imperturbability: the ability to remain calm and unexcited.

36. *levas:* the plural of *lev* (or *leva*), the standard coin in Bulgarian money.

     blabbed: to *blab* is to gossip without thinking of the possible consequences; to reveal secrets by loose talk.

37. *cognac:* French word for brandy obtained from wine made at Cognac, a place in France. Pronounced *kōn-yak.*

38. *made only a very perfunctory toilet:* had dressed hastily and less carefully than if she had been going outside her own home.

     peace: Catherine speaks the word angrily, because she thinks the peace terms are unfavourable to the victors.

     not friendly relations: Petkoff means that although fighting has ended and a peace treaty has been drawn up, the Bulgarians do not intend to be on good terms with the Serbs.

39. *Philippopolis:* a town in central Bulgaria; now called *Plovdiv.*

40. *a Parisian salon:* French fashionable ladies in Paris were accustomed to hold social gatherings attended by beautiful women and handsome men, who were sometimes also learned people and brilliant talkers; *salon* is a French word for a large apartment in a private house or other building.

     Byronism: Many people in Britain and other countries copied the ideas and attitudes of the poet Byron, and such devotion was called *Byronism.*

     jejune: Shaw appears to use the word here to mean 'childish', though the dictionary meaning is 'meagre, scanty, unsatisfying to the mind'. Pronounced *jee-joon.*

41. *Childe Harold:* the hero of a long poem by Byron, *Childe Harold's Pilgrimage*, describing travels in several European countries and referring also to historical persons and events.

     Cossack: The Cossacks were a Turkish tribe who came under Russian rule and were famous as fast-riding cavalry.

42. *ecru:* the Anglicized form of the French word *écru*, meaning *unbleached.*

43. *bagman:* a contemptuous word for a travelling salesman, who

formerly always carried a large bag containing samples of his goods.

43. *Egad:* English colloquial exclamation used as a polite substitute for *By God!* It is seldom heard now.

chargers: name for the horses ridden by military officers.

44. *the seamy side of life:* the darker, sordid, or ugly side.

45. *a knight in a tournament:* in Europe in the Middle Ages noblemen in armour fought in single combat before a seated audience which often included the ladies to whom the knights were devoted. The word *knight* then suggested both *soldier* and *servant of love.*

46. *akimbo:* with hand on hip and elbow extended sideways in line with the body.

the higher love: the exalted and extravagant idea of love between men and women as a spiritual bond with little dependence on physical attraction.

49. *clod of common clay:* Sergius, in an only half-serious bad temper, means that Louka behaves as though she has no soul, but only earthy animal instincts.

50. *flirting:* playful or insincere love-making which goes little further than the paying of complimentary attentions between a young man and a girl.

51. *her fingers itching:* an English idiom meaning that the person has a strong impulse to chastise someone who has behaved annoyingly or badly.

52. *salver:* a flat metal tray on which visitors' name-cards are carried to the host or hostess.

ar'n't they?: Shaw writes it *arnt.* The question is *are they not?*

53. *He raises his eyebrows:* a facial gesture expressing surprise or (sometimes) disapproval.

baulked: hindered, thwarted, or cheated.

54. *forage:* food for the horses.

Act III

57. *hookah:* a smoking-pipe consisting of a vase to hold the lighted tobacco and a long flexible tube with a mouthpiece. The smoke passes through water before it reaches the smoker's mouth.

58. *I sign em: em* is a colloquial contraction for *them;* it is usually
    written *'em.*

    shewing off: displaying something in a conceited manner, or be-
    having conceitedly.

59. *Wholl bet?: Who will bet?* To *bet* (as the word is used here) is to
    put down a sum of money in support of a statement disputed
    by another, who may also put down money. The person who
    is proved right takes all the money. *Wholl* is usually written
    who'll.

    grudge: be unwilling to give or to allow.

    Well, I am d——: Well, I am damned! An oath used in common
    speech, usually to express amazement at some unexpected occur-
    rence. It is sometimes printed with *d——* for *damned,* to avoid
    offence to sensitive readers; but in the play here the dash indi-
    cates that Petkoff is interrupted by Catherine, who disapproves
    of the word she guesses he is about to use.

    hallucinations: things imagined as seen or experienced by persons
    subject to delusions.

    valet: a man's personal male servant.

60. *roused her expectations:* caused her to believe she will receive the
    gift.

    rapt: when a person's attention is so thoroughly given to a par-
    ticular object or thought that he becomes unaware of all else,
    he is said to be *rapt.*

    inflating his chest and thumping it: a gesture of self-satisfaction.

    a thundering good day's work: colloquial emphasis for 'a very good
    day's work'.

    pack them off: send them away immediately.

    they'll have the skin taken off their backs: they will be whipped.

    I'll buy his discharge: I will pay to have him released from the
    army.

61. *You would only splutter at them:* to *splutter* is to make incoherent
    sounds because of timidity or embarrassment, and the splutterer
    often sprays saliva from his mouth.

    capital story: Bluntschli means that it was a very good story.

62. *quite touched:* affected emotionally.

63. *unflinchingly:* steadily; without wavering.

64. *infatuated:* filled with extravagant and uncritical affection.

PAGE

64. *Hand aufs Herz!*: German colloquial expression (*hand on heart*) to emphasize that what the speaker has said is strictly true.

65. *pawned it:* lodged it with a pawnbroker, who lends money on articles which the owner has the right to reclaim later, on repayment of the amount lent with interest added. The article or articles are then said to have been 'redeemed'. The purpose of pawning is to obtain a loan to meet *temporary* financial need.

   phlegmatically: in a cool or indifferent manner; without emotion or excitement. From *phlegm*, a thick semi-fluid substance in the human body and formerly supposed, when in excess, to make a person sluggish and unimpressionable. Pronounced *flem*.

   she flounces away: she moves away with an impatient swing of her body.

   fuming: agitated by suppressed anger.

66. *lips pursed:* lips closed and drawn together into a wrinkled circular shape.

   whacking: slang word for large and bulky.

   disparaging: to *disparage* is to speak slightingly of a person with the intention of giving others a poor opinion of him.

   he has plenty of heart: he is courageous.

67. *dont be so contrary.* don't be so stubborn and disagreeable.

   backing up: supporting or confirming.

68. *youve got to know your place:* you must behave humbly as a servant.

69. *sedately:* here the word indicates that Nicola puts on a hypocritical air of quiet humility.

   slashed . . . and yelled: cut wildly in all directions with their swords and shouted loudly.

70. *the Czar:* title of the former Emperors of Russia.

71. *my affianced bride:* the woman I am bound in honour to marry.

72. *I brook no rivals:* I do not tolerate rivals.

   Switzer: a native of Switzerland.

73. *Stuff! Rubbish!:* idiomatic exclamations meaning that the statement is all nonsense.

74. *A hollow sham:* an empty imposture.

   a blockhead: a dull and stupid person.

   when you cried on: when you agreed.

   now that you cry off: now that you refuse.

75. *no magnetism:* used here to mean *no force of personality*.

75. *Are fresh abysses opening?:* Are new and startling surprises coming?
76. *falls a victim to her sense of humor:* is unable to remain serious.

    nursetending: caring for, as a nurse cares for a baby.
77. *a mutiny brewing:* a mutiny gathering force silently and out of sight before breaking out openly.
78. *dexterously:* neatly and cleverly.
79. *enigmatically:* in a puzzling manner, or with an air of meaning more than the words appear to mean on the surface.
80. *with cool unction:* with hypocritical deference.
81. *testily:* irritably.

    snorts: to *snort* is to express indignation or anger by a sudden forcing of breath through the nose, thus making a sound that suggests explosive emotion.

    She never cared two straws for me: an idiomatic expression for 'She never liked me at all'. Bluntschli speaks deceptively here in order to protect Raina.
82. *hide and seek:* a children's game in which one player runs away and hides, while the others close their eyes until the hidden one gives a signal for the search to begin.

    How the deuce: a polite form of the exclamatory question 'How the devil . . . ?'
83. *sagacity:* discernment or insight or wisdom.
84. *eider-down quilts:* ornamental coverings placed on top of beds to provide extra warmth, and stuffed with very small soft feathers from the breast of the eider duck, an Arctic bird.

    dessert spoons: spoons of medium size used for 'the sweet' or dessert at the end of a meal.

    palatial establishments: large and spacious premises, which in this case are hotels.

    three native languages: French, Italian, and German are spoken in Switzerland.

    Whew!: an exclamation expressing astonishment; more often used by the English to express discomfort in extremely hot weather.
85. *What a man!:* Sergius is filled with half-incredulous admiration for Bluntschli, who seems to him to be almost superhumanly efficient.